Physical Characteristics of the Bichon Frise

(from the American Kennel Club breed standard)

Shoulders: Laid back to somewhat near a 45 degree angle.

Tail: Well plumed, set on level with the topline and curved gracefully over the back so that the hair of the tail rests on the back.

Hindquarters: Of medium bone, well angulated with muscular thighs and spaced moderately wide. The upper and lower thigh are nearly equal in length meeting at a well bent stifle joint. The leg from hock joint to foot pad is perpendicular to the ground.

Color: White, may have shadings of buff, cream or apricot around the ears or on the body.

Size: Dogs and bitches 9.5 to 11.5 inches.

Coat: The undercoat is soft and dense, the outercoat of a coarser and curlier texture. The combination of the two gives a soft but substantial feel to the touch which is similar to plush or velvet and when patted springs back.

Feet: Tight and round, resembling those of a cat and point directly forward, turning neither in nor out.

Bichon Frise

◇

by Juliette Cunliffe

Contents

KENNEL CLUB BOOKS: **BICHON FRISE**
ISBN: 1-59378-221-7

Copyright © 1999 • **Revised American Edition:** Copyright © 2003
Kennel Club Books, Inc., 308 Main Street, Allenhurst, NJ 07711 USA
Cover Design Patented: US 6,435,559 B2 • Printed in South Korea

Photos by Carol Ann Johnson, with additional photos by:
Norvia Behling, Carolina Biological Supply, César Castillo, Doskocil,
Isabelle Français, James Hayden-Yoav, James R. Hayden, RBP,
Dwight R. Kuhn, Dr. Dennis Kunkel, Mikki Pet Products, Phototake,
Jean Claude Revy Dr. Andrew Spielman, Karen Taylor and C. James Webb.

Illustrations by Patricia Peters.

History of the
BICHON FRISE

Theories about the origin of the Bichon Frise vary quite considerably, but the ancestor is generally accepted as being the French breed known as the Barbet, or Water Spaniel. From the Barbet came the name "Barbichon," which was later shortened to become "Bichon." The word "Barbichon" probably evolved from the French word for beard, *barbiche*. All called "Bichon" and originating in the Mediterranean region, four different categories of dog were acknowledged: the Bichon Maltais, Bichon Bolognaise, Bichon Havanais and Bichon Teneriffe, who later became known as the Bichon à Poil Frisé, and, subsequently, as the Bichon Frise we know today.

All of these dogs were appreciated for their disposition and character and were often used as goods with which to barter. So it was that these little dogs traveled widely, being transported from one continent to another by sailors.

Opposite page: The country of origin of the Bichon Frise is probably France. Sailors carried these little dogs around the world as barter and gifts, thus establishing varieties of Bichon-like dogs in different parts of the world.

THE BICHON IN SPAIN

Traveling from Eastern Mediterranean regions to the Balearic Islands, Teneriffe and the Canary Islands, it is usually accepted that it was sailors who introduced the Bichon to Teneriffe. The name of the island was used largely because it enhanced the commercial value of the dog, the very name "Teneriffe" then sounding rather exotic.

The Bichon Teneriffe was particularly popular in Spanish

The Bichon was especially popular in 16th-century Spain among royalty and among artists, who often depicted the dogs in their work.

courts during the 16th century, and painters of the Spanish school often included such dogs in their paintings. Several can be found, particularly in the works of Goya (1746–1828). Goya was both a painter and an etcher and was taken on as court artist to Charles IV in 1789.

THE BICHON IN ITALY
Although known as far back as the 11th century, it was in the 14th century that the Bichon became a particular favorite of the nobility and, as with several other breeds of dog kept in Italy at that time, many were cut into lion trim. They became especially popular in the city of Bologna in northern Italy, and this has become the breed we now know as the Bolognese. However, this breed is much less well known than the Bichon Frise.

In early centuries, Bolognese were highly regarded for their excellent hearing and, although small in size, were often used as watchdogs. In the late 17th century, Bichons Bolognese were sent as gifts from Italian aristocrats to others in France and in Belgium, so spreading their wings still further.

Opposite page: The Bichon Bolognese, shown here, is the Italian Bichon variety.

THE BICHON IN FRANCE
Under Francis I (1515–1547), the Bichon, known as the Bichon Teneriffe, appeared in France and a few decades later became especially popular. It was in the court of Henry III (1547–1589) where this captivating little dog found itself

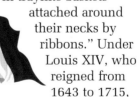

ALL DOLLED UP
These charming little dogs were tenderly cared for by their owners, and the French verb, *bichonner*, which directly translated means "to doll up" or "to pamper," seems to have been evolved from them.

pampered, to the extreme by the standards of the day, wearing ribbons and perfumes.

It was recorded that the French kings and their ladies loved their little white dogs so much that they carried them with them everywhere, "in traylike baskets attached around their necks by ribbons." Under Louis XIV, who reigned from 1643 to 1715, the small dog was designated as the court "pet of choice," reputedly because it was easy to carry about.

Numerous French paintings depict dogs that were Bichon in type, and they also appear frequently in tapestries of earlier

The fabled Bichon Havanese, which derived from the Blanquito de la Habana, is a close relative of the original Bichon Frise.

The famed Blanquito de la Habana derived from the original Spanish Bichon-type dogs and was the basis for the Bichon Havanais, a breed known for the silken texture of its coat.

years, especially those woven in the 15th century. However, it would appear that from 1789, during the French Revolution, they were far less prominent, but they re-emerged with Napoleon III, who declared himself Emperor in 1852.

THE BICHON HAVANAIS

Theories as to the actual origin of the Bichon Havanais are many and varied. This is the breed known today as the Havanese, although, like the Bolognese, it is much less well known than its close relative, the Bichon Frise.

It may be that the Bichon

Havanais descended from the Bolognese and was taken to Argentina by Italians. There it could possibly have been crossed with a small South American Poodle, which effectively would have created another breed.

Another, perhaps more plausible theory, is that the Bichon Havanais instead descended from the Bichon Maltais. These Maltese, as we know them now, were taken to the West Indies by Spaniards. There they became known as the Blanquito de la Habana or Havana Silk Dog, the predecessor of the Havanese we know today.

Two other theories are also worthy of consideration. They may have arrived in Cuba during the time of Spanish colonization and exploration, or Italians may indeed have taken them to Cuba as gifts.

A NON-SPORTING OR TOY DOG?

Early American breeders thought the Bichon should be included in the AKC's Non-Sporting Group rather than the Toy Group, considering that in substance, attitude and type it was better suited to the former. To this day, the Bichon remains in the Non-Sporting Group, rather than being included with Toys as is the case in Britain and other countries.

A photograph of a Vicente Escobar painting that shows a young lady with a Blanquito de la Habana. Escobar was a famous Cuban portrait painter (1757-1854), and this is the earliest (and only) painting of this extinct breed. The original is in the archives of the Salas del Museo Nacional de Cuba in Havana, where it has not been on exhibit for many years.

Whatever their origin, the Bichons Havanais became much adored pets of wealthy Cubans. The Cubans gave these dogs as gifts and somehow they eventually found their way back to Europe.

Although the Bichon Frise we know today is a distinct breed, this has not always been the case. A review in a French magazine published in 1935 actually listed seven names as belonging to what was described as "the same breed name as Bichon." These were the Dog of Tenerife, the Dog of Havana, the Dog of Bologna, the Dog of the Baleares, the Dog of Peru, the Dog of Holland and the Little Lion Dog as described by Buffon, whose works were published in many volumes between 1755 and 1789.

In considering look-alikes, the Poodle does have a fair resemblance to the Bichon Frise. It is possible that an early Bichon relative may have been crossed with a Poodle.

THE LITTLE LION DOG

Because it has been linked with the Bichon Frise in history, it is also of interest to note the connection of the Little Lion Dog, known more familiarly as the Löwchen, or by the French name, Petit Chien Lion. The connection between the two is probably not close. The outlines of the two breeds are quite different in shape, and the coats are not similar. It is highly likely that there is some terrier blood in the Löwchen, and though there may be a little, it is certainly not found to this degree in any other of the true Bichon breeds.

To confuse the issue, the now familiar "lion trim" of the Löwchen had been used on many other

The Löwchen, or Little Lion Dog, historically has been linked with both the Bichon Frise and the Bichon Havanais.

become extinct on the island.

Thankfully, somehow the Coton reappeared at Tulear on the southwestern coast of Madagascar. This was an active trading port and so, once again, the sailors had undoubtedly played their important part in moving another related breed to yet another country.

breeds of dog in the past, and this can only add to one's dilemma when trying to ascertain exactly which breeds were depicted in early representations.

THE COTON DE TULEAR

The little-known Coton de Tulear also cannot go without mention, for its history can be traced back to the Bichon Teneriffe. As trade routes opened up, the Bichon Teneriffe found its way to the island of Reunion in the Indian Ocean. It was here that this little Bichon developed a cotton-like coat, probably the result of a single genetic mutation. This dog was now known as the Coton de Reunion, but eventually the breed was to

THE BICHON'S DECLINE

Despite centuries of having been a pampered pet, towards the close of the 19th century the Bichon seemed to go out of fashion. The reason for this is not easy to comprehend, for in France prosperity was increasing. However, some were still to be found with circuses and fairs, often called "the dog of the street" or sometimes "little sheep dog." Their lives were

The Coton de Tulear's reappearance is a direct result of sailors' bartering Bichon-type dogs for goods, as the breed eventually ended up on the coast of Madagascar in the port of Tulear.

The Coton de Tulear possesses a cotton-like coat and a completely different anatomical structure.

far removed from the luxury the breed had known in earlier years. Sometimes they could be found roaming the streets and were occasional companions to the blind.

THE BREED'S REVIVAL

When the First World War was behind them, a handful of breeders in France and Belgium decided to create a breeding program for the Bichon Teneriffe, or Bichon à Poil Frisé. This, they hoped, would revive the breed and take it beyond the status of the circus or street dog.

Enthusiasm among this small band of dedicated followers was such that by 1933 enough progress had been made for a breed standard to be drawn up. This was written by Mme. Bouctovagniez, who was President of the Toy Club of France, aided by "Friends of the Belgian Breeds." However, when the question of a breed name arose, it was Mme. Nizet de Leemans, head of the Fédération Cynologique Internationale's (FCI) Breed Standards Committee who made this important decision.

The story has been related that at a meeting in 1933 there was heated discussion about what the breed was to be called. In simple desperation, Mme. Nizet de Leemans asked what the breed looked like. It was described as a fluffy little white dog, so she said, without more ado, that it was to be called Bichon Frise, meaning fluffy little dog. So it was that on October 18, 1934, the Bichon Frise was registered in the *Livre des Origines Françaises*. Despite this historical decision, many people continued to use the names Bichon Teneriffe or Bichon à Poil Frisé even into the early 1950s.

INBREEDING

In the years of the breed's revival, there was only a limited supply of foundation stock, so it was understandable that inbreeding had to take place. Inbreeding we define as mating closely related dogs, such as mother to son or father to daughter. Among the early pioneers of the breed were M. et Mme. Bellotte, owners of the Milton prefix, and whose first registered Bichon Frise was born in 1929. To warrant registration, this dog must have been pure-bred for at least four generations.

The Bichon Maltais, more commonly known simply as the Maltese, is the predecessor of the Bichon Havanais and is one of today's most popular breeds.

full American Kennel Club (AKC) recognition. It was accepted for entry in the Miscellaneous Class on September 1, 1971, and was admitted to the AKC Stud Book in October 1972. The breed was allowed regular show classification in the Non-Sporting Group at AKC shows in April 1973. The reason that early American breeders thought the Bichon Frise should be included in the Non-Sporting Group rather than the Toy Group was because they considered that in substance, attitude and type it was better suited to the former.

To those unfamiliar with the official acceptance of "new" breeds in the AKC, the number of years it took to achieve full recognition may seem a very long time, but given the fragmented history of the Bichon, this is actually not the case. Out of interest, the Bichon Frise Club of Canada was formed in 1975.

Although there were Bichons that arrived in America between the 1920s and 1940s, they had

THE BICHON FRISE IN AMERICA

Considering that the Bichon Frise had reached such depths of obscurity until its revival following the First World War, it has certainly had a revival in recent decades! The breed first became active in the US in 1956 and it took a good many years for the Bichon to obtain

entered just as family pets of people who had traveled to Europe and brought them home with them. For the purposes of official introduction to the country, events leading to the entry of the breed to the US must therefore be said to have begun in 1952, when Helene and Français Picault acquired their first Bichon in Dieppe in France. The couple's daughters married Americans and in October 1956 M. et Mme. Picault, and seven Bichons, joined one of their daughters in Milwaukee. Six months later, two more Bichons followed them.

It took the Bichon a while to gain popularity, just as it took Bichon fanciers time to learn the proper ways of grooming and coat care. The breed's image was improved greatly through increased attention to grooming and uniform presentation.

The Picaults had apparently been told that they would make a fortune from breeding Bichons in the US, but all was not as simple as it had been made to appear. Although the breed was thought charming, it was not registered and few puppies were sold in the early days following their arrival. It was in the Midwest that Etoile de Steran Vor produced the first Bichon litter born in the US, this sired by Eddie White de Steren Ver. As time went on the charming little white Bichon wormed its way into the hearts of the American people.

Azelia Gascoigne of Wisconsin had already been involved with other breeds and she bought her first Bichon in 1956, considering that the breed had potential. Another of the early Bichon purchasers was Mrs. Fournier who had bred Collies.

Although progress in bringing the breed to the notice of the public was slow, Mrs. Fournier tried hard to promote the breed and advertised the Bichon in a national dog magazine. Finally, in May of 1964, the formation of a national club was discussed at a meeting in San Diego. This was to be called the Bichon Frise Club of America, Mrs. Gascoigne becoming the club's first President and Mrs. Fournier its Registrar and Secretary.

Through the club, various local groups of Bichon enthusiasts were brought together and the possibility of getting the breed registered with the AKC was on everyone's lips. However, the Bichon was not really taken seriously by other canine enthusiasts in the US. This seems partly to have been because of the breed's history of lack of careful grooming and show presentation on the Continent, where those who traveled had seen the breed.

In 1969, a top professional handler and expert Poodle breeder, Frank Sabella, visited an annual meeting of the breed club, giving his own ideas and suggestions as to how the breed's image could be improved by presentation. He demonstrated how to wash and blow-dry a Bichon, as well as the now important scissoring process and competent handling. Someone else who greatly helped to promote the new image of the breed was Richard Beauchamp, editor of a leading dog magazine. He agreed to join others in the fight for breed recognition and undoubtedly in this he helped greatly.

America was responsible for the first Bichon Frise seen in the show ring in Britain. This was American-bred bitch, Cluneen Lejerdell Tarz Anna, born in June 1973 and exhibited at Leeds Championship Show, England, in May 1974, where she won Best Non Separately Classified.

So, although it took a little time for the Bichon Frise to capture American hearts in the breed's early days on these shores, it certainly flourished in the decades that followed. Now the Bichon is in the top 20 breeds in terms of AKC

The Bichon Frise was finally accepted in 1971, and then fully recognized in 1973, by the American Kennel Club. This occurred more than 100 years after its recognition as a specific breed in Europe.

registrations, with around over 10,000 new registrations each year.

THE BICHON IN BRITAIN

Even as late as the beginning of the 1970s, there were no Bichons known in Britain, although one kept as a pet had been registered with the English Kennel Club in 1957. Even though this dog was not active in any other way, because of its registration the breed could be registered immediately upon arrival in the early 1970s.

The real beginning of the breed in Britain was in 1973 when Mr. and Mrs. J. Sorstein from the US came to live in Britain, bringing with them two Bichons Frises, a dog and a bitch.

The Sorteins' Bichons, Rava's Regal Valor of Reenroy and Jenny-Vive de Carlise, were bred together, and the first litter born in Britain was whelped in 1974. From this litter three puppies returned to the US but two were shown in the UK. The dog, Carlise Cicero of Tresilva, was later to become an Australian champion. This same dog was the sire of Int Ch. Tresilva Don Azur, who made an impact on the breed in Sweden. The mating was repeated in 1975, producing five puppies, helping to form the foundation of other Bichon kennels.

By the 1970s, undoubtedly the charming Bichon Frise had gained many admirers throughout the world and its fame spread. Since then, bloodlines have been

The first Bichon Frise, a pet dog, was registered with The Kennel Club in 1957. It is now a popular breed in the UK as both a companion and a show dog.

exchanged from country to country thanks to numerous exports. The breed is now most certainly one that is taken very seriously. Presentation is first-rate and many high accolades have been achieved, including Best in Show wins and first in the Toy Group at the prestigious Crufts Show in 1999.

Characteristics of the
BICHON FRISE

The Bichon Frise, though fairly small in stature, has a big personality and is great fun to own. Described as "energy and affection in a powder-puff package," this is a remarkably affectionate and intelligent breed with stylish good looks. However, to keep the coat looking as good as it does in the pictures you will find in this book, a certain amount of time and dedication is needed. A coat kept in tip-top condition usually has attention paid to it every day, so this is a very important consideration when adopting a Bichon Frise.

A long-lived breed, the Bichon Frise can often live to 15 or 16 years of age, so this is another factor that must be seriously contemplated before deciding that this is really the breed for you. Clearly, when taking a new pet into your home, the most important aim will be that the dog remains with you for life.

The Bichon has risen rapidly in the popularity stakes and currently there are thousands of

Once you have fallen in love with the Bichon Frise, you will be enamored for life! Because the Bichon Frise is small, intelligent, lovable and well behaved, it is easy to keep more than one. Who can resist?

new puppies registered with the American Kennel Club each year. This puts the breed in the top 20 most popular of all breeds registered in the US.

PHYSICAL CHARACTERISTICS

Because of the Bichon's profuse curly white coat, the physical structure concealed beneath can come as something of a surprise to the uninitiated. This is an exceptionally sound breed, not exaggerated structurally in any way. Although the Bichon is actually just a little longer than high, this is not immediately apparent because of the coat that stands off the body, creating an overall powder-puff appearance.

Thanks to the breed's sound construction, it is capable of moving with great ease, and many Bichons can be quite bouncy around the home. Bichons are quite capable of taking part in agility trials. No weight clause is specified in the standard for this breed, but weight usually falls somewhere between 10–18 lb.

Apart from the coat, the head of the Bichon surely stands out as quite unforgettable, looking, as it does, like three lumps of coal on a background of snowy white. It is the grooming of the coat that creates the rounded appearance of the head, for underneath the furnishings the skull and muzzle shape are not

FACE STAINING
Face staining on the white Bichon is of genuine concern to many owners. Sometimes staining can be caused by blocked tear ducts or ingrown eyelashes, but most of the time it is primarily a cosmetic problem. There are now many products available to remedy tear staining.

at all extraordinary.

The head is set on a fairly long, arched neck, so that the head is carried high and proudly, conveying a thoroughly smart little dog with a big personality inside. The tail, too, gives an indication of the character of this little breed, for it is usually carried raised and curved gently over the back.

PERSONALITY

We can describe the breed as a gay, happy, lively little dog, its temperament friendly and outgo-

The standard describes the Bichon Frise as a "gay, happy, lively little dog"...and that he is! Combine his wonderful personality with his stunning looks, and it's hard to think of a better choice for a pet.

home environment where he can take part in family life, and all the "goings on" around him will be readily absorbed by his intelligent mind.

WHAT THE BICHON ENJOYS

The Bichon is a breed that enjoys training and learns well. Activities that he is capable of learning are obedience, therapy work, agility and even the odd trick or two. However, the Bichon does not take well to overly firm training and some seem to learn best when training takes the form of a little game. He is always ready to accept treats, so care must be taken that he does not inadvertently gain excess weight as a result of his training exercises.

When selecting a collar and leash for training, the chain collar should be avoided for it can too easily become entangled in the hair and may indeed damage the hair around the neck.

COLOR AND COAT

Coat color and coat presentation on the Bichon are very important, so owners of the breed must be prepared to put in a good deal of work to keep it in tip-top condition, never looking dirty or unkempt. A white coat will only stay white if bathed frequently.

The color of the Bichon's coat is always white, but cream or apricot markings are accept-

ing. The AKC standard goes on to call the breed, "gentle mannered, sensitive, playful and affectionate. A cheerful attitude is the hallmark of the breed and one should settle for nothing less."

A real extrovert, the Bichon is rarely shy or nervous and is a veritable joy to live with. He thrives on being the center of attention. In history, this little dog has lived as a companion animal, and that is exactly what he should be for he appreciates all the comforts of home. A Bichon is happiest living in a

able up to 18 months of age. Under the white coat, the pigment should ideally be dark, and black, blue or beige markings can often be found on the skin.

The white of the coat contrasts strikingly against the black nose pigment and dark, round eyes with black pigment surrounding them. The skin that surrounds the eyes is usually black or dark gray. These areas are called halos, and this dark skin coloring accentuates the eyes and enhances the expression of this delightful dog. Even the pads of the feet are black, and the nails should preferably be black too, although these are quite difficult to find.

Most Bichons are kept in a rather jaunty-looking trim, for this is how the breed is best known today, although this has not always been the case. Indeed it was the development of the breed's coat presentation that helped the Bichon to rise to fame. The coat style is undoubtedly one of the greatest attractions of the breed.

Coat texture is extremely important. The fine, silky coat has soft, corkscrew curls and is 3–4 inches in length. The Bichon also has a soft, dense undercoat. For the show ring, the coat is trimmed to the natural outline of the body, rounded off and never cut so short as to create an overly trimmed or squared-off appearance. Pets are frequently kept with shorter coat on body and legs, but retaining the length on head, ears and tail to give a characteristic appearance.

The dead coat of the Bichon does not drop but is replaced, so as a result it must be combed out, otherwise knots and tangles will result. It is also very important in this breed that the coat is

The Bichon Frise is much more than a lap dog. He thrives on exercise, running, jumping and playing games with his owner. As a matter of fact, sufficient exercise is necessary for his health.

thoroughly groomed out before bathing; if not, the bathing procedure will only result in more tangles developing.

On the head, the beard and moustache are left longer, as are the ears, giving an overall rounded impression. The head coat is never trimmed so short that the breed loses its characteristic powder-puff appearance, and the coat on the tail, too, is left somewhat longer.

BICHONS WITH CHILDREN

Provided that parents have trained their children to treat dogs gently, being neither rough nor aggressive, most Bichons thoroughly enjoy playing with youngsters. It must, though, be understood that young children should always be supervised when in the company of dogs in order that accidents do not happen, however unintentional they might be.

BICHONS WITH OTHER FAMILY PETS

Always when one animal is introduced to another, careful supervision is essential. Most Bichons are quite prepared to associate with other animals, but a lot understandably depends on the personality of the other. An older dog or cat may not take readily to a newcomer to the household, although others accept them well. When a Bichon does find another canine or feline friend, usually the relationship is lasting and sincere. Indeed one of the dangers, in view of the Bichon's rather special coat, is mutual grooming that can play havoc with the coat, especially behind the ears!

HEALTH CONSIDERATIONS

In general this is a healthy, hardy little dog but, as in so many other breeds, certain health problems arise in the Bichon Frise. However, it is thanks to the dedication of breeders that these have been discovered and largely rectified. If owners are aware of the problems that can occur, they are undoubtedly in a position to deal with them in the best manner possible. Some problems are genetic and are carried via heredity, but others are not.

SKIN ALLERGIES

Some Bichons are prone to skin allergies, but they can often be

TIPPING THE SCALES

The easiest method of weighing your Bichon is on the bathroom scales. First weigh yourself alone, then a second time while holding the dog in your arms. Deduct one from the other to obtain the accurate weight of your Bichon. (This procedure inevitably encourages the owner's dieting as well... "Is my subtraction really that rusty?"!)

Bichons Frises are, as a general rule, very healthy and happy pets. A newly acquired puppy should be examined by your vet to be sure that he is healthy and sound.

kept under control with a carefully considered diet. The allergy is often noticed as "hot spots" on the skin, despite there being no sign of external parasites. A low-protein diet often seems to suit skin troubles.

It is often extremely difficult to ascertain the cause of the allergy. There are many possibilities, ranging from the sitting-room carpet, the shampoo used when bathing and, quite frequently, certain grasses and molds. In cases of skin allergy, it is a good idea to change shampoo, conditioning rinse and any other coat sprays used, for these are perhaps the easiest items to eliminate before looking further if necessary. It goes without saying that your Bichon must be kept free of external parasites such as fleas and ticks.

LEG PROBLEMS

Bichons are known to suffer from trouble with the knee joints, known as luxating patella, though of course only a few are affected. A luxated patella simply means a "slipped kneecap." Reliable breeders have their breeding stock checked regularly by a vet, which has helped to reduce the incidence. Another important factor is that a dog should not be overweight as this is likely to exacerbate the problem. Many dogs with luxating patella live with the problem without experiencing pain, but surgery is necessary in some extreme cases.

Another problem currently

URINE LUCK!

To take a urine sample to your vet for analysis, the easiest way is to catch the urine in a large, clean bowl and then transfer this to a bottle. Owners who have spent many fruitless hours attempting to get their dogs or bitches to urinate directly into a bottle will be yellow with envy to discover this little trick.

being investigated in Bichons is one affecting the hip joint. Hip dysplasia, the most common of all canine orthopedic problems, does not have a high incidence in the Bichon.

BLADDER STONES

Although found infrequently in the Bichon, bladder stones can sometimes cause a problem, as they are found more often in small breeds than in larger ones. Symptoms include frequent passing of urine, blood in the urine, straining to pass water, general weakness, depression and loss of appetite. Bladder stones occur more frequently in females than males.

Urgent veterinary attention is necessary, for stones in the bladder can lead to irreparable kidney damage and life can be lost as a result. In many cases, stones can be dissolved by a

The Bichon Frise is a lot of spirit in a small package. With routine health care, your Bichon will remain happy, healthy and active throughout his life.

special diet under veterinary supervision, but certain types require surgical removal.

TEETH

As with many of the smaller breeds, some Bichons lose their teeth at a relatively early age. It is therefore important to pay close attention to the care of teeth and gums so that they remain as healthy as possible, thereby preventing decay, infection and resultant early loss.

Infection in the gums may not just stop there. The bacteria from this infection is carried through the bloodstream, the result of which can be disease of liver, kidney, heart, and the joints. This is all the more reason to realize that efficient dental care is of utmost importance throughout a dog's life.

EYES

A problem that has only recently been revealed in the Bichon Frise is that of cataracts,

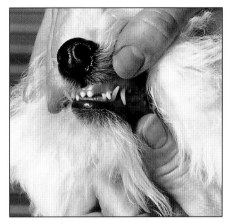

Puppy teeth are fine and sharp. You can start a dental-care routine with your Bichon when he is a pup.

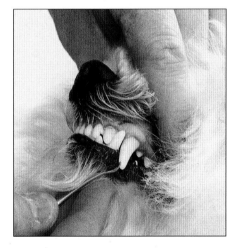

Be certain that the adult's teeth have emerged properly with no deciduous teeth remaining.

THE BENEFITS OF YOGURT

At the first sign of any minor infection, the author has often found that live yogurt, administered orally, is of great benefit. This sometimes has the effect of rectifying the problem almost immediately, before a course of antibiotics becomes necessary.

and the mode of inheritance is currently being researched. At this early stage of discovery, various schemes are currently implemented in different countries. It is therefore advisable for new owners to make inquiries as to which tests are available at the current time.

Initially it would be sensible to contact the secretary of a

Because the Bichon Frise's coat is such an important part of the dog's appearance, daily attention to tear stains is critical. Pet shops have specially made cosmetics and cleaners for tear-stain removal.

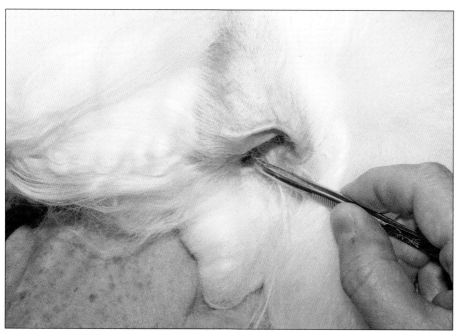

Excess hair growing in the dog's ear canal should be plucked out. With instruction and practice on your part, this can be a painless procedure for the dog.

breed club to ascertain the current situation and obtain up-to-date information. Details of secretaries can be obtained from the American Kennel Club.

Because of the hair around the eye of the Bichon, the eyeball can be irritated. This can result in conjunctivitis and is very likely to cause an excess of tear production. This, in consequence, causes tear staining below the eye, something often noticed on white and light-colored dogs. Clearly, attention is therefore necessary to keep the eyes clean and this should be a routine aspect of grooming this breed.

EARS

Because the Bichon's ears hang close to the head and are well covered with flowing hair in accordance with the breed standard, there can be lack of ventilation. It is therefore important that ears are checked regularly and that excess hair is carefully plucked from inside the ear to avoid infection arising.

Signs of an infected ear include a brown smelly discharge that leads to the ear's becoming red, inflamed and sore. At this stage, the dog will scratch at the ear and may hold his head on one side because of the pain.

The American Kennel Club breed standard for the Bichon Frise is effectively a "blue-print" for the breed. It sets down the various points of the dog in words, enabling a visual picture to be conjured up in the mind of the reader. However, this is more easily said than done. Not only do standards vary from country to country, but people's interpretations of breed standards vary also. It is this difference of interpretation which makes judges select different dogs for top honors, for their opinions differ as to which dog most closely fits the breed standard. That is not to say that a good dog does not win regularly under different judges, nor that an inferior dog may rarely even be placed at a show, at least not among quality competition.

The breed standard given here is that authorized by the American Kennel Club; it was approved on October 11, 1988 and became effective on November 30 of that same year. The standard is comprehensive, and so is reasonably self-explanatory. However, as with most breeds there are variances between the standard used in the US and that used in Britain. For example, the AKC standard tells readers about the breed's undercoat, whereas the British standard makes no mention of it, although the Bichon most certainly has one!

Another notable difference is that qualification in Britain that the standard only accepts white, cream or apricot markings up to 18 months of age.

THE AMERICAN KENNEL CLUB STANDARD FOR THE BICHON FRISE

General Appearance: The Bichon Frise is a small, sturdy, white powder puff of a dog whose merry temperament is evidenced by his plumed tail carried jauntily over

At dog shows, the judge uses the breed standard as the guide to evaluate each dog entered in the competition.

the back and his dark-eyed inquisitive expression. This is a breed that has no gross or incapacitating exaggerations and therefore there is no inherent reason for lack of balance or unsound movement. Any deviation from the ideal described in the standard should be penalized to the extent of the deviation. Structural faults common to all breeds are as undesirable in the Bichon Frise as in any other breed, even though such faults may not be specifically mentioned in the standard.

Size, Proportion, Substance: *Size*: Dogs and bitches 9.5 to 11.5 inches are to be given primary preference. Only where the comparative superiority of a specimen outside this range clearly justifies it should greater latitude be taken. In no case, however, should this latitude ever extend over 12 inches or under 9 inches. The minimum limits do not apply to puppies. *Proportion*: The body from the forward-most point of the chest to the point of rump is one-quarter longer than the height at the withers. The body from the withers to lowest point of chest represents one-half the distance from withers to ground. *Substance*: Compact and of medium bone throughout; neither coarse nor fine.

Head: *Expression*: Soft, dark-eyed, inquisitive, alert. Eyes are round, black or dark brown and are set in

Bichons competing in dog shows are not actually compared against one another; each dog is compared against the "perfect" specimen of the breed described in the breed standard.

the skull to look directly forward. An overly large or bulging eye is a fault as is an almond shaped, obliquely set eye. Halos, the black or very dark brown skin surrounding the eyes, are necessary as they accentuate the eye and enhance expression. The eye rims themselves must be black. Broken pigment, or total absence of pigment on the eye rims produce a blank and staring expression, which is a definite fault. Eyes of any color other than black or dark brown are a very serious fault and

The breed has certainly changed since its introduction into the US. Originally, the Bichon Frise was longer back and lower on leg. Grooming techniques, too, have evolved over the years, and were less precise in the early years. These dogs would have been correct in the 1970s.

Gradually backs became shorter and legs longer. Grooming became more sculptured, but the head trim featured longer ear fringes and beard, and the topknot was rounded. These dogs would have been correct in the 1980s.

must be severely penalized. Ears are drop and are covered with long flowing hair. When extended toward the nose, the leathers reach approximately halfway the length of the muzzle. They are set on slightly higher than eye level and rather forward on the skull, so that when the dog is alert they serve to frame the face. The skull is slightly rounded, allowing for a round and forward looking eye. The stop is slightly accentuated. *Muzzle:* A properly balanced head is three parts muzzle to five parts skull, measured from the nose to the stop and from the stop to the occiput. A line drawn between the outside corners of the eyes and to the nose will create a near equilateral triangle. There is a slight degree of chiseling under the eyes, but not so much as to result in a weak or snipey foreface. The lower jaw is strong. The nose is prominent and always black. Lips are black, fine, never drooping. Bite is scissors. A bite which is undershot or overshot should be severely penalized. A crooked or out of line tooth is permissible, however, missing teeth are to be severely faulted.

Neck, Topline and Body: The arched neck is long and carried proudly behind an erect head. It blends smoothly into the shoulders. The length of neck from occiput to withers is approximately one-third the distance from forechest to buttocks. The topline is level except for a slight, muscular arch over the loin. *Body:* The chest is well developed and wide enough to allow free and unrestricted movement of the front legs. The lowest point of the chest extends at least to the elbow. The rib cage is moderately sprung and extends back to a short and muscular loin. The forechest is well pronounced and protrudes slightly forward of the point of shoulder. The underline has a moderate tuck-up. Tail is well plumed, set on level with the topline and curved gracefully over the back so that the hair of the tail rests on the back. When the tail is extended toward the head it reaches at least halfway to the withers. A low tail set, a tail carried perpendicularly to the back, or a tail which droops behind is to be severely penalized. A corkscrew tail is a very serious fault.

Forequarters: *Shoulders:* The shoulder blade, upper arm and forearm are approximately equal in length. The shoulders are laid back to somewhat near a 45° angle. The upper arm extends well back so the elbow is placed directly below the withers when viewed from the side. Legs are of medium bone; straight, with no bow or curve in the forearm or wrist. The elbows are held close to the body. The pasterns slope slightly from the vertical. The dewclaws may be removed. The feet are tight and round, resembling those of a cat and point directly forward, turning neither in nor out. Pads are black. Nails are kept short.

Hindquarters: The hindquarters are of medium bone, well angulated

In profile, a modern dog, showing correct balance, type and structure, groomed for show-ring presentation in the 21st century.

Headstudy of correct structure, type, showing desirable dark pigment and eye color. This trim, emphasizing an overall rounded appearance, is the current style for breed presentation.

When bathed and brushed, it stands off the body, creating an overall powder puff appearance. A wiry coat is not desirable. A limp, silky coat, a coat that lies down, or a lack of undercoat are very serious faults. *Trimming:* The coat is trimmed to reveal the natural outline of the body. It is rounded off from any direction and never cut so short as to create an overly trimmed or squared off appearance. The furnishings of the head, beard, mustache, ears and tail are left longer. The longer head hair is trimmed to create an overall rounded impression. The topline is trimmed to appear level. The coat is long enough to maintain the powder puff look which is characteristic of the breed.

Color: Color is white, may have shadings of buff, cream or apricot around the ears or on the body. Any color in excess of 10% of the entire coat of a mature specimen is a fault and should be penalized, but color of the accepted shadings should not be faulted in puppies.

Gait: Movement at a trot is free, precise and effortless. In profile the forelegs and hind legs extend equally with an easy reach and drive that maintain a steady topline. When moving, the head and neck remain somewhat erect and as speed increases there is a very slight convergence of legs toward the center line. Moving

with muscular thighs and spaced moderately wide. The upper and lower thigh are nearly equal in length meeting at a well bent stifle joint. The leg from hock joint to foot pad is perpendicular to the ground. Dewclaws may be removed. Paws are tight and round with black pads.

Coat: The texture of the coat is of utmost importance. The undercoat is soft and dense, the outer coat of a coarser and curlier texture. The combination of the two gives a soft but substantial feel to the touch which is similar to plush or velvet and when patted springs back.

away, the hindquarters travel with moderate width between them and the foot pads can be seen. Coming and going, his movement is precise and true.

Temperament: Gentle mannered, sensitive, playful and affectionate. A cheerful attitude is the hallmark of the breed and one should settle for nothing less.

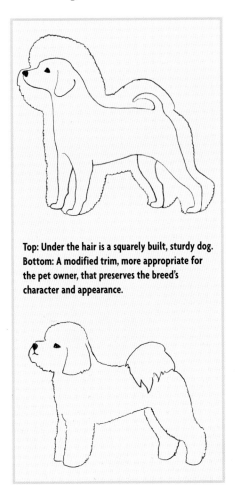

Top: Under the hair is a squarely built, sturdy dog. Bottom: A modified trim, more appropriate for the pet owner, that preserves the breed's character and appearance.

AUTHOR'S NOTE

Although a great deal can be learned from the breed standard, only by seeing good-quality, typical specimens can you really learn to appreciate the breed's merits. Therefore, readers interested in showing their Bichons should watch other dogs being exhibited, and learn as much as possible from established breeders and exhibitors.

It is very helpful to attend judges' seminars, often hosted by breed clubs. Here the finer points of the breed can be explained fully and discussed. There is usually a dog, or perhaps several, available for demonstration purposes, and there may even be an opportunity for participants to feel beneath the coat for the structure of the animal.

Trimming and skillful artistic presentation can hide a multitude of sins on coated breeds, especially the Bichon. The standard states quite clearly the correct set on and carriage of the ears, as well as their length. Good judges will always take care that presentation has not superficially remedied structural faults.

The Bichon is a sound little dog, and thus should it remain. Both breeders and judges should always be aware of structural faults that may not be apparent because of an expertly presented coat. Conversely, it must also be borne in mind that the appearance of a well-constructed dog can be marred by poor presentation.

BICHON FRISE

You have probably decided on a Bichon Frise as your choice of pet following a visit to the home of a friend or acquaintance, where you have seen an adorable Bichon looking clean, pretty and wandering happily around the house, joining politely in the family fun. However, as a new owner, you must realize that a good deal of care, commitment and careful training goes into raising a bois-

terous puppy so that your pet turns into a well-behaved adult.

In deciding to take on a new puppy, you will be committing yourself to around 15 years of responsibility. No dog should be discarded after a few months, or even a few years, after the novelty has worn off. Instead, your Bichon should be joining your household to spend the rest of his days with you.

This young Bichon shows his owner a little "puppy love." In no time, your puppy will be affectionate and loving with you.

Although temperamentally a Bichon Frise is much easier to look after than many other breeds, you will still need to carry out a certain amount of training. Unlike some of the larger breeds, the Bichon will not respond well to overly strict training. Instead you will need to take a firm but gentle approach in order to get the very best out of your pet.

A Bichon generally likes to be clean around the house, but you will need to teach your puppy what is and is not expected. You will need to be consistent in your instructions; it is no good accepting certain behavior one day and not the next. Not only will your puppy simply not understand, he will be utterly confused. Your Bichon will want to please you, so you will need to demonstrate clearly how he is to achieve this.

Before making your commitment to a new puppy, do also think carefully about your future vacation plans. If you have thought things through carefully, discussed the matter thoroughly with all members of your family, hopefully you will have come to the right decision. If you decide that a Bichon should join your family this will hopefully be a happy, long-term relationship for all parties concerned.

Although small, puppy teeth are very sharp. Pups should be given strong, safe chew devices made especially for dogs.

ARE YOU PREPARED?

Unfortunately, when a puppy is bought by someone who does not take into consideration the time and attention that dog ownership requires, it is the puppy who suffers when he is either abandoned or placed in a shelter by a frustrated owner. So all of the "homework" you do in preparation for your pup's arrival will benefit you both. The more informed you are, the more you will know what to expect and the better equipped you will be to handle the ups and downs of raising a puppy. Hopefully, everyone in the household is willing to do his part in raising and caring for the pup. The anticipation of owning a dog often brings a lot of promises from excited family members: "I will walk him every day," "I will feed him," "I will house-train him," etc., but these things take time and effort, and promises can easily be forgotten once the novelty of the new pet has worn off.

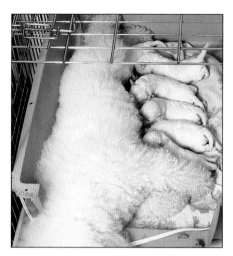

BUYING A BICHON FRISE PUPPY

Although you may be looking for a Bichon as a pet, rather than a show dog, this does not mean that you want a dog that is in any way "second-rate." A caring breeder will have brought up the entire litter of puppies with the same amount of dedication, and a puppy destined for a pet home should be just as healthy as one that hopes to end up in the show ring.

Because you have carefully selected this breed, you will want a Bichon Frise that is a typical specimen, both in looks and temperament. In your endeavors to find such a puppy, you will have to select the breeder with care. The American Kennel Club will be able to give you names of contacts within Bichon breed clubs. These people can possibly put you in touch with breeders who may have puppies for sale. However, although they can point you in the right direction, it will be up to you to do your homework.

For potential buyers, it is a good idea to visit a show so that you can see quality specimens of the breed. This will also give you an opportunity to meet breeders who will probably be able to answer some of your queries. In addition, you will get some idea about which breeders appear to take most care of their stock, and which are likely to have given their puppies the best possible start in life.

When buying your puppy, you will need to know about vaccinations, those already given and those still due. It is important that any injections already given

TEMPERAMENT COUNTS

Your selection of a good puppy can be determined by your needs. A show potential or a good pet? It is your choice. Every puppy, however, should be of good temperament. Although show-quality puppies are bred and raised with emphasis on physical conformation, responsible breeders strive for equally good temperament. Do not buy from a breeder who concentrates solely on physical beauty at the expense of personality.

At eight weeks of age, the puppies should be fully weaned and fairly well socialized with each other, and probably will have met some people other than the breeder. Their individual personalities will be evident by this time as well.

PUPPY APPEARANCE

Your puppy should have a well-fed appearance but not a distended abdomen, which may indicate worms or incorrect feeding, or both. The body should be firm, with a solid feel. The skin of the abdomen should be pale pink and clean, without signs of scratching or rash. Check the hind legs to make certain that dewclaws were removed, if any were present at birth.

by a veterinarian have documentation to prove this. A worming routine is also vital for any young puppy, so the breeder should be able to tell you exactly what treatment has been given, when it has been administered, and how you should continue.

Clearly when selecting a puppy, the one you choose must be in good condition. The coat should look healthy and there should be no discharge from eyes

Three puppies eagerly await your attention, but the fourth has found something more interesting. Which kind of dog do you want? You'll probably find that the puppy chooses you much in the same way that you choose him!

or nose. Ears should also be clean, and with absolutely no sign of parasites. Check that there is no rash on the skin, and of course the puppy you choose should not have evidence of loose motions.

As in several other breeds, a few Bichon Frise puppies have umbilical hernias, which can be a

PEDIGREE VS. REGISTRATION CERTIFICATE

Too often new owners are confused between these two important documents. Your puppy's pedigree, essentially a family tree, is a written record of a dog's genealogy of three generations or more. The pedigree will show you the names as well as performance titles of all the dogs in your pup's background. Your breeder must provide you with a registration application, with his part properly filled out. You must complete the application and send it to the AKC with the proper fee. Every puppy must come from a litter that has been AKC-registered by the breeder, born in the USA and from sire and dam that are also registered with the AKC.

The seller must provide you with complete records to identify the puppy. The AKC requires that the seller provide the buyer with the following: breed; sex, color and markings; date of birth; litter number (when available); names and registration numbers of the parents; breeder's name; and date sold or delivered.

seen as a small lump on the belly where the umbilical cord was attached. Clearly it is preferable not to have such a hernia on any puppy, but you should check for this at the outset and if there is one you should discuss the seriousness of this with the breeder. Most umbilical hernias are safe, but your vet should keep an eye on this in case an operation is warranted.

When buying a pup, always insist that you see the puppy's dam and, if possible, the sire. However, frequently the sire will not be owned by the breeder of the litter, but a photograph may be available for you to see. Ask if the breeder has any other of the puppy's relations that you could meet. For example, there may be an older half-sister or -brother and it would be interesting for you to see how he/she has turned out, the eventual size, coat quality, temperament and so on.

Be sure, too, that if you decide to buy a puppy, all relevant documentation is provided at the time of sale. You will need a copy of the pedigree, preferably American Kennel Club registration documents, vaccination certificates and a feeding chart so that you know exactly how the puppy has been fed and how you should continue. Some careful breeders provide their puppy buyers with a small amount of food. This prevents the risk of an upset tummy, allowing for a gradual change of diet if that particular brand of food is not locally available.

COMMITMENT OF OWNERSHIP
After considering all of these factors, you have most likely already made some very important decisions about selecting your puppy. You have chosen a Bichon Frise, which means that you have decided which characteristics you want in a dog and what type of dog will best fit into your family and lifestyle. If you have selected a breeder, you have gone a step further—you have done your research and found a responsible, conscientious person who breeds quality Bichons Frises and who should be a reliable source of help as you and your puppy adjust to life together. If you have observed a litter in action, you have obtained a first-hand look at the dynamics of a puppy "pack" and, thus, you should learn about each pup's

Puppies and adults need different diets. Discuss the best diet for your puppy with your breeder.

TIME TO GO HOME
Breeders rarely release puppies until they are eight to ten weeks of age. This is an acceptable age for most breeds of dog, excepting toy breeds, which are not released until around 12 weeks, given their petite sizes. If a breeder has a puppy that is 12 weeks of age or older, it is likely well socialized and house-trained. Be sure that it is otherwise healthy before deciding to take it home.

Are you ready for the commitment that accompanies one of these fluffy little angels?

YOUR SCHEDULE...

If you lead an erratic, unpredictable life, with daily or weekly changes in your work requirements, consider the problems of owning a puppy. The new puppy has to be fed regularly, socialized (loved, petted, handled, introduced to other people) and, most importantly, allowed to go outdoors for house-training. As the dog gets older, he can be more tolerant of deviations in his feeding and relief schedule.

individual personality—perhaps you have even found one that particularly appeals to you.

However, even if you have not yet found the Bichon Frise puppy of your dreams, observing pups will help you learn to recognize certain behavior and to determine what a pup's behavior indicates about his temperament. You will be able to pick out which pups are the leaders, which ones are less outgoing, which ones are confident, which ones are shy, playful, friendly, aggressive, etc. Equally as important, you will learn to recognize what a healthy pup should look and act like. All of these things will help you in your search, and when you find the Bichon Frise that was meant for you, you will know it!

Researching your breed, selecting a responsible breeder and observing as many pups as possible are all important steps on the way to dog ownership. It may seem like a lot of effort...and you have not even taken the pup home yet! Remember, though, you cannot be too careful when it comes to deciding on the type of dog you want and finding out about your prospective pup's background. Buying a puppy is not—or *should* not be—just another whimsical purchase. This is one instance in which you actually do get to choose your own family! You may be thinking that buying a puppy should be fun—it should not be so serious and so much work. Keep in mind that your puppy is not a cuddly stuffed toy or decorative ornament, but a creature that will become a real member of your family. You will come to realize that, while buying a puppy is a pleasurable and exciting endeavor, it is not something to be taken lightly. Relax…the fun will start when the pup comes home!

Always keep in mind that a puppy is nothing more than a baby in a furry disguise…a baby who is virtually helpless in a human world and who trusts his owner for fulfillment of his basic needs for survival. In addition to food, water and shelter, your pup needs care, protection, guidance and love. If you are not prepared to commit to this, then you are not prepared to own a dog.

"Wait a minute," you say. "How hard could this be? All of my neighbors own dogs and they seem to be doing just fine. Why should I have to worry about all of this?" Well, you should not

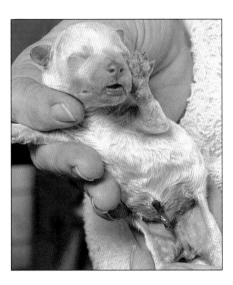

A new-born Bichon Frise, only a few minutes old.

worry about it; in fact, you will probably find that once your Bichon Frise pup gets used to his new home, he will fall into his place in the family quite naturally. But it never hurts to emphasize the commitment of dog ownership. With some time and patience, it is really not too difficult to raise a curious and exuberant Bichon Frise pup to be a well-adjusted and well-mannered adult dog—a dog that could be your most loyal friend.

PREPARING PUPPY'S PLACE IN YOUR HOME

Researching your breed and finding a breeder are only two aspects of the homework you will have to do before bringing your Bichon Frise puppy home. You will also have to prepare your home and family for the new addition.

ARE YOU A FIT OWNER?

If the breeder from whom you are buying a puppy asks you a lot of personal questions, do not be insulted. Such a breeder wants to be sure that you will be a fit provider for his puppy.

Most Bichons Frises quickly adapt to their crates.

Much as you would prepare a nursery for a newborn baby, you will need to designate a place in your home that will be the puppy's own. How you prepare your home will depend on how much freedom the dog will be allowed. Whatever you decide, you must ensure that he has a place that he can "call his own."

When you bring your new puppy into your home, you are bringing him into what will become his home as well. Obviously, you did not buy a puppy so that he could take control of your house, but in order for a puppy to grow into a stable, well-adjusted dog, he has to feel comfortable in his surroundings. Remember, he is leaving the warmth and security of his mother and littermates, as well as the familiarity of the only place he has ever known, so it is important to make his transition as easy as possible. By preparing a place in your home for the puppy, you are making him feel as welcome as possible in a strange new place. It should not take him long to get used to it, but the sudden shock of being transplanted is somewhat traumatic for a young pup. Imagine how a small child would feel in the same situation—that is how your puppy must be feeling. It is up to you to reassure him and to let him know, "Little angel, you are going to like it here!"

WHAT YOU SHOULD BUY

CRATE
To someone unfamiliar with the use of crates in dog training, it may seem like punishment to

PET INSURANCE

Just like you can insure your car, your house and your own health, you likewise can insure your dog's health. Investigate a pet insurance policy by talking to your vet. Depending on the age of your dog, the breed and the kind of coverage you desire, your policy can be very affordable. Most policies cover accidental injuries, poisoning, and thousands of medical problems and illnesses, including cancers. Some carriers also offer routine care and immunization coverage.

shut a dog in a crate, but this is not the case at all. Most breeders advocate crate training, and trainers recommend the crate as a preferred tool for show puppies as well as pet puppies. Crates are not cruel—crates have many humane and highly effective uses in dog care and training. For example, crate training is a very popular and very successful housebreaking method. A crate can keep your dog safe during travel and, perhaps most importantly, a crate provides your dog with a place of his own in your home. It serves as a "doggie bedroom" of sorts—your Bichon Frise can curl up in his crate when he wants to sleep or when he just needs a break. Many dogs sleep in their crates overnight. When lined with soft bedding and his favorite toy, a crate becomes a

Photo courtesy of Doskocil.

Your local pet shop should carry a complete assortment of crates and kennels. Get one large enough for the full-grown Bichon Frise.

cozy pseudo-den for your dog. Like his ancestors, he too will seek out the comfort and retreat of a den—you just happen to be providing him with something a little more luxurious than his early ancestors enjoyed.

As far as purchasing a crate, the type that you buy is up to you. It will most likely be one of the two most popular types: wire or fiberglass. There are advantages and disadvantages to each type. For example, a wire crate is more open, allowing the air to flow through and affording the dog a view of what is going on around

THE RIDE HOME

Taking your dog from the breeder to your home in a car can be a very uncomfortable experience for both of you. The puppy will have been taken from his warm, friendly, safe environment and brought into a strange new environment—an environment that moves! Be prepared for loose bowels, urination, crying, whining and even fear biting. With proper love and encouragement when you arrive home, the stress of the trip should quickly disappear.

The crate you select should be large enough so that your Bichon Frise can comfortably stand, turn around and lie down when he is fully grown.

take the place of the leaves, twigs, etc., that the pup would use in the wild to make a den; the pup can make his own "burrow" in the crate. Although your pup is far removed from his den-making ancestors, the denning instinct is still a part of his genetic makeup. Second, until you bring your pup home, he has been sleeping amid the warmth of his mother and littermates, and while a blanket is not the same as a warm, breathing body, it still provides heat and something with which to snuggle. You will want to wash your pup's bedding frequently in case he has

him while a fiberglass crate is sturdier. Both can double as car-travel crates, providing protection for the dog. For air travel, however, only the fiberglass crate is acceptable. The size of the crate is another thing to consider. Puppies do not stay puppies forever—in fact, sometimes it seems as if they grow right before your eyes. A medium-small crate will be necessary for a full-grown Bichon Frise, who stands approximately 11 inches high.

BEDDING

A crate pad and a small blanket in the dog's crate will help the dog feel more at home. This will

CRATE TRAINING TIPS

During crate training, you should partition off the section of the crate in which the pup stays. If he is given too big an area, this will hinder your training efforts. Crate training is based on the fact that a dog does not like to soil his sleeping quarters, so it is ineffective to keep a pup in a crate that is so big that he can eliminate in one end and get far enough away from it to sleep. Also, you want to make the crate den-like for the pup. Blankets and a favorite toy will make the crate cozy for the small pup; as he grows, you may want to evict some of his "roommates" to make more room. It will take some coaxing at first, but be patient. Given some time to get used to it, your pup will adapt to his new home-within-a-home quite nicely.

PHOTO COURTESY OF MIKKI PET PRODUCTS.

Pet shops offer a wide selection of suitable dog toys that your Bichon Frise will welcome. Never offer your dog toys that are manufactured for children as they may be dangerous to a teething puppy.

an accident in his crate, and replace or remove any blanket that becomes ragged and starts to fall apart.

Toys

Toys are a must for dogs of all ages, especially for curious playful pups. Puppies are the "children" of the dog world, and what child does not love toys? Chew toys provide enjoyment to both dog and owner—your dog will enjoy playing with his favorite toys, while you will enjoy the fact that they distract him from your expensive shoes and leather sofa. Puppies love to chew; in fact, chewing is a physical need for pups as they are teething, and everything looks appetizing! The full range of your possessions—from your favorite hairbrush to your new Oriental rug—are fair

The crate can serve as the Bichon Frise's bedroom. Just leave the door open—once used to it, your Bichon wil go into his crate to rest without being told.

game in the eyes of a teething pup. Puppies are not all that discerning when it comes to finding something to literally "sink their teeth into"—everything tastes great!

Breeders advise owners to resist stuffed toys, because they can become de-stuffed in no time. The overly excited pup may ingest the stuffing, which is neither digestible nor nutritious.

Similarly, squeaky toys are quite popular, but must be avoided for the Bichon Frise. Perhaps a squeaky toy can be used as an aid in training, but not for free play. If a pup "disembowels" one of these, the small plastic squeaker inside can be dangerous if swallowed. Monitor the condition of all your pup's toys carefully and get rid of any that have been chewed to the point of becoming potentially dangerous.

Be careful of natural bones, which have a tendency to splinter into sharp, dangerous pieces. Also be careful of rawhide, which can turn into pieces that are easy to swallow or into a mushy mess on your carpet.

LEASH
A nylon leash is probably the best option as it is the most resistant to puppy teeth should your pup take a liking to chewing on his leash. Of course, this is a habit that should be nipped in the bud, but if your pup likes to chew on his leash, he has a very slim

TOYS, TOYS, TOYS!
With a big variety of dog toys available, and so many that look like they would be a lot of fun for a dog, be careful in your selection. It is amazing what a set of puppy teeth can do to an innocent-looking toy; so, obviously, safety is a major consideration. Be sure to choose the most durable products that you can find. Hard nylon bones and toys are a safe bet, and many of them are offered in different scents and flavors that will be sure to capture your dog's attention. It is always fun to play a game of fetch with your dog, and there are balls and flying discs that are specially made to withstand dog teeth.

Supply your Bichon with something appropriate to chew. "Zoey" looks happy with her treat, but "Rumors" wants one, too!

chance of being able to chew through the strong nylon. Nylon leashes are also lightweight, which is good for a young Bichon Frise who is just getting used to the idea of walking on a leash. For everyday walking and safety purposes, the nylon leash is a good choice. As your pup grows up and gets used to walking on the leash, you may want to purchase a flexible leash. These leashes allow you to extend the length to give the dog a broader area to explore or to shorten the length to keep the dog close to you.

COLLAR

Your pup should get used to wearing a collar all the time since you will want to attach his ID tags to it. You have to attach the leash to something! A lightweight nylon collar is a good choice; make sure that it fits snugly enough so that the pup cannot wriggle out of it, but is loose enough so that it will not be uncomfortably tight around the pup's neck. You should be able to fit a finger between the pup and the collar. It may take some time for your pup to get used to wearing the collar, but soon he will not even notice that it is there. Never use chain collars on your Bichon. Chain choke collars are made for training, but should only be used by an experienced handler and not on small or coated dogs.

Most trainers recommend using a lightweight nylon leash for your Bichon. Pet shops offer dozens of choices for collars and leashes, in different styles, colors and lengths.

FOOD AND WATER BOWLS

Your pup will need two bowls, one for food and one for water. You may want two sets of bowls, one for inside and one for outside, depending on where the dog will be spending time. Stainless steel or sturdy plastic bowls are popular choices. Plastic bowls are more chewable. Dogs tend not to chew on the steel variety, which can be sterilized. It is important to buy sturdy bowls since anything is in danger of being chewed by puppy teeth and you do not want your dog to be constantly chewing apart his bowl (for his safety and for your wallet!).

Cleaning Supplies

Until a pup is house-trained, you will be doing a lot of cleaning. Accidents will occur, which is okay in the beginning because the puppy does not know any better. All you can do is be prepared to clean up any accidents. Old rags, paper towels, newspapers and a safe disinfectant are good to have on hand.

Provide your Bichon with feeding and watering bowls. These bowls can be constructed of sturdy plastic, ceramic, clay or stainless steel.

Beyond the Basics

The items previously discussed are the bare necessities. You will find out what else you need as you go along—grooming supplies, flea/tick protection, baby gates to partition a room, etc. These things will vary depending on your situation but it is important that you have everything you need to feed and make your Bichon Frise comfortable in his first few days at home.

PUPPY-PROOFING YOUR HOME

Although the dog you are bringing into your home will be fairly small, and therefore probably less troublesome than a larger dog, there will undoubtedly be a period of settling in. This can be great fun, but you must be prepared for mishaps around the home during the first few weeks of your life together. It will be important that precious ornaments are kept well out of harm's way, and you will have to think twice about where you place hot

PHOTO COURTESY OF MIKKI PET PRODUCTS.

CHOOSE AN APPROPRIATE COLLAR

The **BUCKLE COLLAR** is the standard collar used for everyday purposes. Be sure that you adjust the buckle on growing puppies. Check it every day. It can become too tight overnight! These collars can be made of leather or nylon. Attach your dog's identification tags to this collar.

The **CHOKE COLLAR** is designed for training. It is constructed of highly polished steel so that it slides easily through the stainless steel loop. The idea is that the dog controls the pressure around his neck and he will stop pulling if the collar becomes uncomfortable. A choke chain is not recommended for a coated breed like the Bichon Frise.

The **HALTER** is for a trained dog that has to be restrained to prevent running away, chasing a cat and the like. Considered the most humane of all collars, it is frequently used on smaller dogs on which collars are not comfortable.

To prepare for your new puppy, you should have proper bedding, safe chew devices for teething, puppy food and a good book to show you the way.

cups of coffee or anything breakable. Accidents can and do happen, so you will need to think ahead so as to avoid these.

Responsible law-abiding dog owners pick up their dogs' droppings whenever they are in public. Pooper-scooper devices make the job quick and easy.

Keeping your Bichon safe inside the home requires "puppy-proofing," which means taking precautions that your pup will not get into anything he should not get into and that there is nothing within his reach that may harm him should he sniff it, chew it, inspect it, etc. This probably seems obvious since, while you are primarily concerned with your pup's safety, at the same time you do not want your belongings to be ruined. Breakables should be placed out of reach if your dog is to have full run of the house. If he is to be limited to certain places within the house, keep any potentially dangerous items in the "off-limits" areas. An electrical cord can pose a danger should the puppy decide to taste it—and who is going to convince a pup that it would not make a great

chew toy? Cords should be fastened tightly against the wall. If your dog is going to spend time in a crate, make sure that there is

nothing near his crate that he can reach if he sticks his curious little nose or paws through the openings. Just as you would with a child, keep all household cleaners and chemicals where the pup cannot get to them.

It is also important to make sure that the outside of your home is safe. Of course your puppy should never be unsupervised, but a pup let loose in the yard will want to run and explore, and he should be granted that freedom. Do not let a fence give you a false sense of security; you would be surprised how crafty (and persistent) a dog can be in figuring out how to dig under and squeeze his way through small holes, or to jump or climb over a fence. The remedy is to make the fence high enough so that it really is impossible for your dog to get over it (about 6 feet should suffice), and well embedded into the ground. Be sure to repair or secure any gaps in the fence. Check the fence periodically to ensure that it is in good shape and make repairs as needed; a very determined pup may return to the same spot to "work on it" until he is able to get through.

FIRST TRIP TO THE VET

You have picked out your puppy, and your home and family are ready. Now all you have to do is collect your Bichon Frise from the breeder and the fun begins, right? Well…not so fast. Something else you need to prepare is your pup's first trip to the vet. Perhaps the breeder can recommend someone in the area who specializes in Bichons Frises or coated breeds, or maybe you know some other Bichon Frise owners who can suggest a good vet. Either way, you should have an appointment arranged for your pup before you pick him up and plan on taking him for an examination before bringing him home.

The pup's first visit will consist of an overall examination

GARDEN SAFETY

Many plants can be toxic to dogs. If you see your dog carrying a piece of vegetation in his mouth, approach him in a quiet, disinterested manner, avoid eye contact, pet him and gradually remove the plant from his mouth. Alternatively, offer him a treat and maybe he'll drop the plant on his own accord.

Examine your grass and landscaping before bringing your puppy home. Be sure no toxic plants are growing in your own garden. Many varieties of plants have leaves, stems or flowers that are toxic if ingested, and you can depend on a curious puppy to investigate them. Ask your vet for information on poisonous plants or research them at your library.

to make sure that the pup does not have any problems that are not apparent to you. The veterinarian will also set up a schedule for the pup's vaccinations; the breeder will inform you of which ones the pup has already received and the vet can continue from there.

INTRODUCTION TO THE FAMILY
Everyone in the house will be excited about the puppy's coming home and will want to pet him and play with him, but it is best to keep the introductions low-key so as not to overwhelm the puppy. He is apprehensive already. It is the first time he has been separated from his mother and the breeder, and the ride to your home is likely the first time he has been in a car. The last thing you want to do is smother him, as this will only frighten him further. This is not to say that human contact is not extremely necessary at this stage, because this is the time when a connec-

tion between the pup and his human family is formed. Gentle petting and soothing words should help console him, as well as just putting him down and letting him explore on his own (under your watchful eye, of course).

The pup may approach the family members or may busy himself with exploring for a while. Gradually, each person should spend some time with the pup, one at a time, crouching down to get as close to the pup's level as possible and letting him sniff his hands and petting him gently. He definitely needs human attention and he needs to be touched—this is how to form an immediate bond. Just remember that the pup is experiencing a lot of things for the first time, at the same time. There are new people, new noises, new smells and new things to investigate: so be gentle, be affectionate and be as comforting as you can be.

YOUR PUP'S FIRST NIGHT HOME
You have traveled home with your new charge safely in his crate or on a family member's lap. He's been to the vet for a thorough checkup, he's been weighed, his papers examined; perhaps he's even been vaccinated and wormed as well. He's met the family, licked the whole family, including the excited children and the less-than-happy cat. He's

CHEMICAL TOXINS
Scour your garage for potential puppy dangers. Remove weed killers, pesticides and antifreeze materials. Antifreeze is highly toxic and just a few drops can kill a puppy or an adult dog. The sweet taste attracts the animal, who will quickly consume it from the floor or pavement.

explored his area, his new bed, the yard and anywhere else he's been permitted. He's eaten his first meal at home and relieved himself in the proper place. He's heard lots of new sounds, smelled new friends and seen more of the outside world than ever before.

That was just the first day! He's worn out and is ready for bed...or so you think!

It's puppy's first night and you are ready to say "Good night"—keep in mind that this is puppy's first night ever to be sleeping alone. His dam and littermates are no longer at paw's length and he's a bit scared, cold and lonely. Be reassuring to your new family member. This is not the time to spoil him and give in to his inevitable whining.

Puppies whine. They whine to let the others know where they are and hopefully to get company out of it. Place your pup in his new bed or crate in his room and

All members of the family should handle gently the new Bichon Frise puppy as part of the socialization process.

SKULL & CROSSBONES

Thoroughly puppy-proof your house before bringing your puppy home. Never use cockroach or rodent poisons or plant fertilizers in any area accessible to the puppy. Avoid the use of toilet cleaners. Most dogs are born with "toilet-bowl sonar" and will take a drink if the lid is left open. Also keep the trash secured and out of reach.

close the door. Mercifully, he may fall asleep without a peep. When the inevitable occurs, ignore the whining: he is fine. Be strong and keep his interest in mind. Do not allow your heart to become guilty and visit the pup. He will fall asleep.

Many breeders recommend placing a piece of bedding from his former homestead in his new bed so that he recognizes the scent of his littermates. Others still advise placing a hot water bottle in his bed for warmth. This latter may be a good idea provided the pup doesn't attempt to suckle—he'll get good and wet and may not fall asleep so fast.

Puppy's first night can be somewhat stressful for the pup and his new family. Remember that you are setting the tone of nighttime at your house. Unless you want to play with your pup every night at 10 p.m., midnight and 2 a.m., don't initiate the habit. Your family will thank you, and so will your pup!

PREVENTING PUPPY PROBLEMS

SOCIALIZATION

Now that you have done all of the preparatory work and have helped your pup get accustomed to his new home and family, it is about time for you to have some fun! Socializing your Bichon Frise pup gives you the opportunity to show off your new friend, and your pup gets to reap the benefits of being an adorable furry creature that people will want to pet and, in general, think is absolutely precious!

Besides getting to know his new family, your puppy should be exposed to other people, animals and situations, but of course he must not come into close contact with dogs you don't know well until his course of injections is fully complete. This will help him become well adjusted as he grows up and less prone to being timid or fearful of the new things he will encounter. Your pup's socialization began at the breeder's but now it is your responsibility to continue it. The socialization he receives up until the age of 12 weeks is the most critical, as this is the time when he forms his impressions of the outside world. The breeder is especially careful during the eight-to-ten-week period, also known as the fear period. The interaction he receives during this time should be gentle and reas- suring. Lack of socialization can manifest itself in fear and aggres- sion as the dog grows up. He needs lots of human contact, affection, handling and exposure to other animals.

Once your pup has received

FINANCIAL RESPONSIBILITY

Grooming tools, collars, leashes, crate, dog beds and, of course, toys will be expenses to you when you first obtain your pup, and the cost will continue throughout your dog's lifetime. If your puppy damages or destroys your possessions (as most puppies surely will!) or something belonging to a neighbor, you can calculate additional expense. There is also flea and pest control, which every dog owner faces more than once. You must be able to handle the financial responsibility of owning a dog.

How can you refuse these "puppy-dog" eyes? Whether it's pleading for more treats or the "I-didn't-do-it" look, be consistent in enforcing the rules with your young Bichon.

his necessary vaccinations, feel free to take him out and about (on his leash, of course). Walk him around the neighborhood, take him on your daily errands, let people pet him, let him meet other dogs and pets, etc. Puppies do not have to try to make friends; there will be no shortage of people who will want to introduce themselves. Just make sure that you carefully supervise each meeting. If the neighborhood children want to say hello, for example, that is great—children and

WHO'S THE BOSS

The majority of problems that are commonly seen in young pups will disappear as your dog gets older. However, how you deal with problems when he is young will determine how he reacts to discipline as an adult dog. It is important to establish who is boss (hopefully it will be you!) immediately when you are first bonding with your dog. This bond will set the tone for the rest of your life together.

pups most often make great companions. Sometimes an excited child can unintentionally handle a pup too roughly, or an overzealous pup can playfully nip a little too hard. You want to make socialization experiences positive ones. What a pup learns during this very formative stage will impact his attitude toward future encounters. You want your dog to be comfortable around everyone. A pup that has a bad

The Bichon Frise usually is a good choice for a multiple-pet household; this is a friendly breed that gets along well with other animals.

PUP MEETS WORLD

Thorough socialization includes not only meeting new people but also being introduced to new experiences such as riding in the car, having his coat brushed, hearing the television, walking in a crowd—the list is endless. The more your pup experiences, and the more positive the experiences are, the less of a shock and the less frightening it will be for your pup to encounter new things.

FEEDING TIPS

You will probably start feeding your pup the same food that he has been getting from the breeder; the breeder should give you a few days' supply to start you off. Although you should not give your pup too many treats, you will want to have puppy treats on hand for coaxing, training, rewards, etc. Be careful, though, as a small pup's calorie requirements are relatively low and a few treats can add up to almost a full day's worth of calories without the required nutrition.

experience with a child may grow up to be a dog that is shy around or aggressive toward children.

CONSISTENCY IN TRAINING

Dogs, being pack animals, naturally need a leader, or else they try to establish dominance in their packs. When you bring a dog into your family, the choice of who becomes the leader and who becomes the "pack" is entirely up to you! Your pup's intuitive quest for dominance, coupled with the fact that it is

Children may want to try their hand at showing the family Bichon. Local shows are fun and a good way to get started.

nearly impossible to look at an adorable Bichon Frise pup, with his "puppy-dog" eyes and not cave in, give the pup almost an unfair advantage in getting the upper hand! A pup will definitely test the waters to see what he can and cannot do. Do not give in to those pleading eyes—stand your ground when it comes to disciplining the pup and make sure that all family members do the same. It will only confuse the pup when Mother tells him to get off the couch when he is used to sitting up there with Father to watch the nightly news. Avoid discrepancies by having all members of the household decide on the rules before the pup even comes home...and be consistent in enforcing them! Early training shapes the dog's personality, so you cannot be unclear in what you expect.

THE COCOA WARS

Chocolate contains the chemical thebromine, which is poisonous to dogs, although "chocolates" especially made for dogs are safe (as they don't actually contain chocolate) but not recommended. Any item that encourages your dog to enjoy the taste of cocoa should be discouraged. You should also exercise caution when using mulch in your garden. This frequently contains cocoa hulls, and dogs have been known to die from eating the mulch.

COMMON PUPPY PROBLEMS

The best way to prevent puppy problems is to be proactive in stopping an undesirable behavior as soon as it starts. The old saying "You can't teach an old dog new tricks" does not necessarily hold true, but it is true that it is much easier to discourage bad behavior in a young developing pup than to wait until the pup's bad behavior becomes the adult dog's bad habit. There are some problems that are especially prevalent in puppies as they develop.

NIPPING

As puppies start to teethe, they feel the need to sink their teeth into anything available...unfortunately that includes your fingers, arms, hair and toes. You may find this behavior cute for the first five seconds...until you feel just how sharp those puppy teeth are. This is something you want to discourage immediately and consistently with a firm "No!" (or whatever number of firm "Nos" it takes for him to understand that you mean business). Then replace your finger with an appropriate chew toy. While this behavior is merely annoying when the dog is young, it can become dangerous as your Bichon Frise's adult teeth grow in and his jaws develop, and he continues to think it is okay to gnaw on human appendages. Your Bichon Frise does not mean any harm with a friendly nip, but he also does not know his own strength.

CRYING/WHINING

Your pup will often cry, whine, whimper, howl or make some type of commotion when he is left alone. This is basically his way of calling out for attention to make sure that you know he is there and that you have not forgotten about him. He feels insecure when he is left alone, when you are out of the house and he is in his crate or when you are in another part of the house and he cannot see you. The noise he is making is an expression of the anxiety he feels at being alone, so he needs to be taught that being alone is okay. You are not actually training the dog to stop making noise, you are training him to feel comfortable when he is alone and thus removing the need for him to make the noise. This is where the crate filled with cozy bedding and a toy comes in handy. You want to know that he is safe when you are not there to supervise, and

you know that he will be safe in his crate rather than roaming freely about the house. In order for the pup to stay in his crate without making a fuss, he needs to be comfortable in his crate. On that note, it is extremely important that the crate is never used as a form of punishment, or the pup will have a negative association with the crate.

Accustom the pup to the crate in short, gradually increasing time intervals in which you put him in the crate, maybe with a treat, and stay in the room with him. If he cries or makes a fuss, do not go to him, but stay in his sight. Gradually he will realize that staying in his crate is okay without your help, and it will not be so difficult for him when you are not around. You may want to leave the radio on softly when you leave the house; the sound of human voices may be comforting to him.

Puppies thrive in an environment with structure. Be consistent in your training techniques, your house rules and your schedule to train your Bichon puppy.

IN DUE TIME

It will take at least two weeks for your puppy to become accustomed to his new surroundings. Give him lots of love, attention, handling, frequent opportunities to relieve himself, a diet he likes to eat and a place he can call his own.

Quality dog foods are more costly than generic brands but the nutritional value is well worth the added expense.

DIETARY AND FEEDING CONSIDERATIONS

Today the choices of food for your Bichon Frise are many and varied. There are simply dozens of brands of food in all sorts of flavors and textures, ranging from puppy diets

FOOD PREFERENCE

Selecting the best dry dog food is difficult. There is no majority consensus among veterinary scientists as to the value of nutrient analysis (protein, fat, fiber, moisture, ash, cholesterol, minerals, etc.). All agree that feeding trials are what matter, but you also have to consider the individual dog. The dog's weight, age and activity level, and what pleases his taste, all must be considered. It is probably best to take the advice of your veterinarian. Every dog's dietary requirements vary, even during the lifetime of a particular dog.

If your dog is fed a good dry food, it does not require supplements of meat or vegetables. Dogs do appreciate a little variety in their diets, so you may choose to stay with the same brand but vary the flavor. Alternatively, you may wish to add a little flavored stock to give a difference to the taste.

to those for seniors. There are even hypoallergenic and low-calorie diets available. Because your Bichon Frise's food has a bearing on coat, health and temperament, it is essential that the most suitable diet is selected for a Bichon Frise of his age. It is fair to say, however, that even dedicated owners can be somewhat perplexed by the enormous range of foods available. Only understanding what is best for your dog will help you reach a valued decision.

Dog foods are produced in three basic types: dry, semi-moist and canned. Dry foods are useful for the cost-conscious for overall they tend to be less expensive than semi-moist or canned. These contain the least fat and the most preservatives. In general canned foods are made up of 60–70% water, while semi-moist ones often contain so much sugar that they are perhaps the least preferred by owners, even though their dogs seem to like them.

When selecting your dog's diet, three stages of development must be considered: the puppy stage, the adult stage and the senior stage.

PUPPY STAGE

Puppies instinctively want to suck milk from their mother's teats and a normal puppy will exhibit this behavior from just a few moments following birth. If puppies do not attempt to suckle within the first half-hour or so, they should be encouraged to do so by placing them on a nipple, having selected ones with plenty of milk. This early milk supply is important in providing colostrum to protect the

You will feed puppy food to your new charge until around ten months of age.

puppies during the first eight to ten weeks of their lives. Although a mother's milk is much better than any milk formula, despite there being some excellent ones available, if the puppies do not feed the breeder will have to handfeed them. For those with less experience, advice from a veterinarian is important so that you feed not only the right quantity of milk but also that of correct quality, fed at suitably frequent intervals, usually every two hours during the first few days of life.

Puppies should be allowed to nurse from their mother for about the first six weeks, although from the third or fourth week small portions of suitable solid food can be introduced. Most breeders like to introduce alternate milk

TEST FOR PROPER DIET

A good test for proper diet is the color, odor and firmness of your dog's stool. A healthy dog usually produces three semi-hard stools per day. The stools should have no unpleasant odor. They should be the same color from excretion to excretion.

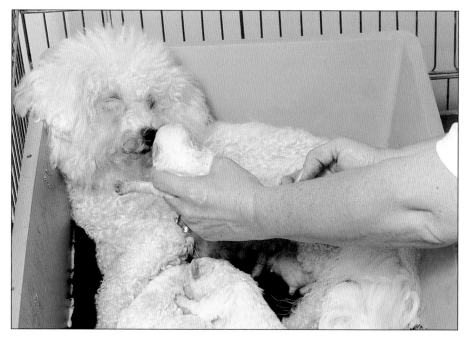

Puppies should nurse from their mothers for about the first six weeks of their lives, with small bits of solid food introduced around three or four weeks.

and meat meals initially, building up to weaning time.

By the time the puppies are seven or a maximum of eight weeks old, they should be fully weaned and fed solely on a proprietary puppy food. Selection of the most suitable, good-quality diet at this time is essential for a puppy's fastest growth rate is during the first year of life. Veterinarians are usually able to offer advice in this regard and, although the frequency of meals will have been reduced over time, change of diet will have been followed according to the manufacturer's instructions.

Puppy and junior diets should be well balanced for the needs of your dog, so that except in certain circumstances additional vitamins, minerals and proteins will not be required.

ADULT DIETS

A dog is considered an adult when he has stopped growing, so in general the diet of a Bichon will have been changed to an adult one by 10 or 12 months of age, sometimes sooner depending on your selection of diet. There are many specially prepared diets available, but do keep in mind that adult Bichons seem to thrive best on a light diet with fairly low protein content. This applies particularly to those that have been spayed or castrated. It is important that you select the food best suited to your dog's needs, for active dogs will require a different diet than those leading a more sedate life.

SENIOR DIETS

As dogs get older, their metabolism changes. The older dog usually exercises less, moves more slowly and sleeps more. This change in lifestyle and physiological performance requires a change in diet. Since these changes take place slowly, they might not be recognizable. What is easily recognizable is weight gain. By continuing to feed your dog an adult-maintenance diet when he is slowing down metabolically, your dog will gain

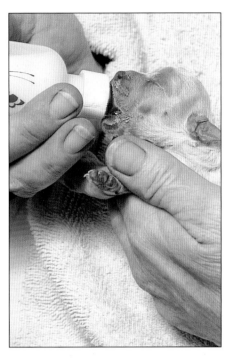

If for some reason the puppy will not suckle, or the dam will not allow it to feed, the breeder has the job of handfeeding the puppy.

weight. Obesity in an older dog compounds the health problems that already accompany old age.

As your dog gets older, few of his organs function up to par. The kidneys slow down and the intestines become less efficient. These age-related factors are best handled with a change in diet and a change in feeding schedule to give smaller portions that are more easily digested.

There is no single best diet for every older dog. While many dogs do well on light or senior diets, other dogs do better on puppy diets or other special premium diets such as lamb and rice. Be sensitive to your senior Bichon

GRAIN-BASED DIETS

Some less expensive dog foods are based on grains and other plant proteins. While these products may appear to be attractively priced, many breeders prefer a diet based on animal proteins and believe that they are more conducive to your dog's health. Many grain-based diets rely on soy protein, which may cause flatulence (passing gas).

There are many cases, however, when your dog might require a special diet. These special requirements should only be recommended by your veterinarian.

A Worthy Investment

Veterinary studies have proven that a balanced high-quality diet
pays off in your dog's coat quality, behavior and activity level.
Invest in premium brands for the maximum payoff with your dog.

Frise's diet and this will help control other problems that may arise with your old friend.

WATER
Just as your dog needs proper nutrition from his food, water is an essential "nutrient" as well. Water keeps the dog's body properly hydrated and promotes normal function of the body's systems. During housebreaking, it is necessary to keep an eye on how much water your Bichon Frise is drinking, but once he is reliably trained he should have access to clean fresh water at all times. Make sure that the dog's water bowl is clean, and change the water often, making sure that water is always available for your dog, especially if you feed dry food.

EXERCISE
Although a Bichon Frise is small, all dogs require some form of exercise, regardless of breed. A sedentary lifestyle is as harmful to a dog as it is to a person. The Bichon Frise is a fairly active breed that enjoys exercise, but you don't have to be an Olympic athlete! Regular walks, play sessions in the yard and letting the dog run free in an enclosed area under your supervision are sufficient forms of exercise for the Bichon Frise. For more ambitious, you will find that your Bichon Frise also enjoys long walks, an

occasional hike or even a swim!

Bear in mind that an overweight dog should never be suddenly over-exercised; instead he should be allowed to increase exercise slowly. Not only is exercise essential to keep the dog's body fit, it is essential to his mental well-being. A bored dog will find something to do, which often manifests itself in some type of destructive behavior. In this sense, it is essential for the owner's mental well-being as well!

GROOMING
Your Bichon Frise will need to be groomed regularly, so it is essential that short grooming sessions be introduced from a very early age. From the very beginning, a

Don't let the Bichon's small size fool you...he needs exercise and he loves to run and play!

few minutes each day should be set aside, the duration building up slowly as the puppy matures and the coat grows in length and thickness. Your puppy should be taught to stand on a solid surface for grooming, a suitable table on which the dog will not slip. Never, under any circumstances, leave your Bichon alone on a table, for he may all too easily jump off and harm himself.

When the puppy is used to standing on the table, you will probably find it useful to teach him to be rolled over onto his side. This you will do by grasping his front and back legs on the opposite side of your own body, then gently placing him down by leaning over him for reassurance. To begin, just stroke his tummy so that he looks upon this new routine as something highly pleasurable. Then, when you know he is comfortable with this, introduce a few gentle brush strokes. Be sure not to hurt him at all at this stage, for this would cause him to associate this routine with discomfort.

Your Bichon Frise must be groomed regularly. It is a process that will take some practice on the part of both you and the dog.

This may take a little getting used to both for you and your puppy, but if your Bichon learns to lie down on his side you will more easily be able to groom him in all the awkward places. You will both be glad you had a little patience to learn this trick from the very start!

As puppies, Bichons have only a single coat, which is soft in texture. By adulthood a double coat develops, enabling the coat to stand out from the body. This change to double coat can be a difficult time, for particular care is needed to avoid tangles being formed as the puppy coat grows out. A fully mature coat is usually significantly developing by around one year of age.

ROUTINE GROOMING

To achieve the lovely powder-puff coat for which the breed is so well known, it is important to keep it clean and to groom regularly, even between baths. Owners who keep their Bichons as pets rather than as show dogs will still need to pay attention to the coat on a daily basis, and a trip to a professional groomer every four or five weeks is the best option. It is important not to let a Bichon's coat get out of hand, but a Bichon rescue society will always be willing to offer advice if an owner is having problems with the coat. Telephone numbers of breed rescue societies are usually avail-

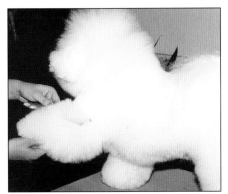

"Line brushing" involves grooming one section of the coat at a time, starting with the legs.

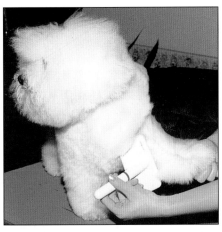

A good-quality slicker brush is the first choice of many professional groomers.

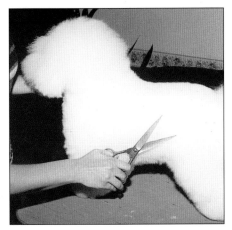

The sculpted look of the show Bichon Frise depends on the skill of the groomer's scissors.

The desired round appearance of the head is achieved by careful trimming and a steady hand.

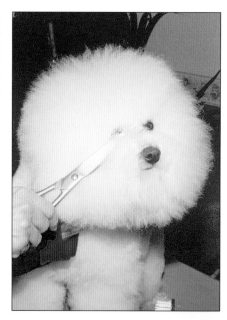

The hair on the pads of the feet should be trimmed to avoid any hairballs from causing the feet to spread.

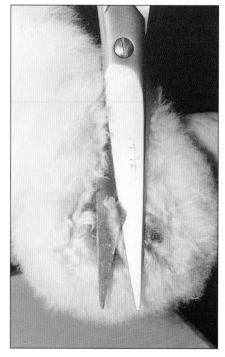

able through the American Kennel Club or through a Bichon breed club.

Each owner has his own favorite way of grooming his dog, and hopefully other owners with whom you come into contact will freely pass on some of their tips. Some like to begin with combing, but others feel it is necessary to use the slicker brush first of all. You will undoubtedly develop your own particular routine with the progression of time.

What is called "line-brushing" is generally considered the most efficient method. This involves holding down one section of hair while gently brushing through the adjacent section using a good-quality slicker brush. Use of a poor-quality, cheap slicker brush can too easily damage the skin. It is essential to brush right through to the skin, otherwise mats will continue to form and will be left behind in the coat.

It is important to cover brushing of the entire dog in a systematic way. Most people begin with feet and legs, working over the body and lastly the head, starting above the eyes and working backward toward the skull. The tail plume on a Bichon is important and therefore this should be treated with great care in order not to remove too much hair.

Unless you are one of the owners who prefers to commence

by using a comb, when brushing is completed a metal comb is used to puff up the coat, thereby creating the familiar powder-puff effect. You may choose to start at the front or the back, but be systematic. Use light strokes to lift up the coat. This is done by putting the teeth of the comb into the coat and then lifting, constantly repeating this pattern. Take care grooming the tummy and under the "arm-pits," for these areas are especially sensitive. Finally, gently comb through the ears and beard, and of course the tail.

Any powder used must be thoroughly brushed out of the coat prior to exhibition, and again it is a matter of personal preference whether or not powder is used. Certainly some owners find that a little powder in the coat helps avoid removing too much coat when grooming, but others use it only for cleaning stains.

BATHING AND DRYING
How frequently you decide to bathe your Bichon Frise will depend very much on whether yours is a show dog or a pet. Show dogs are usually bathed before every show, which may be as frequently as once a week. Pet dogs are usually bathed less frequently.

As with grooming, every owner has his own preference as to how best to bathe, but ideally

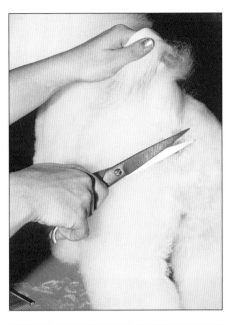

Be careful not to cut the tail plume when scissoring the dog's rear.

Brushing should be gentle and thorough, especially after bathing. The coat should never be left to air-dry on its own.

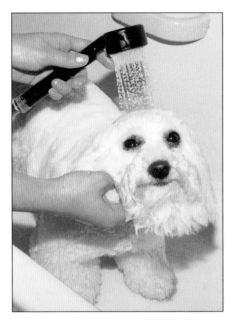

The Bichon's coat should be thoroughly wet before the shampoo is applied.

There are special shampoos for dogs, and even some specially made for white dogs.

the coat should have been groomed through before bathing. I like to stand my own dogs on a non-slip mat in the bathtub, then wet the coat thoroughly using a shower. It is imperative first to test the water temperature on your own hand. Use a good-quality shampoo designed especially for dogs; indeed some are now especially suitable for the white coat of a Bichon. Always stroke the shampoo into the coat rather than rub, so as not to create knots. When this has been thoroughly rinsed out, apply a canine conditioner in the same manner, then rinse again until the water runs clear. Many people like to use a baby shampoo on the head to avoid irritation to the eyes, and some like to plug the ears with cotton to avoid water getting inside them. Personally, I use neither of these, but taking care especially in that area, I have

SOAP IT UP

The use of human soap products like shampoo, bubble bath and hand soap can be damaging to a dog's coat and skin. Human products are too strong; they remove the protective oils coating the dog's hair and skin that make him water-resistant. Use only shampoo made especially for dogs. You may like to use a medicated shampoo, which will help to keep external parasites at bay.

BATHING BEAUTY

Once you are sure that the dog is thoroughly rinsed, squeeze the excess water out of his coat with your hand and dry him with an heavy towel. You may choose to use a blow dryer on his coat or just let it dry naturally. In cold weather, never allow your dog outside with a wet coat.

There are "dry bath" products on the market, which are sprays and powders intended for spot cleaning, that can be used between regular baths if necessary. They are not substitutes for regular baths, but they are easy to use for touch-ups as they do not require rinsing.

All traces of shampoo should be thoroughly rinsed from the Bichon Frise's coat and then the dog should be wrapped in a heavy towel and lifted from the bath.

never encountered problems. Finally, lift your Bichon carefully out of the bath, wrapped in a clean towel. Undoubtedly your dog will want to shake—so be prepared!

Drying can be done on whichever table you use for the grooming process. Work systematically, applying warm air from the hair-dryer. According to your preference, you may use your comb or slicker brush to help separate the hair as it dries, always encouraging the coat upwards and outwards.

SCISSORING

When scissoring the coat, you will need to use a long-bladed sharp scissors, so take extreme care not

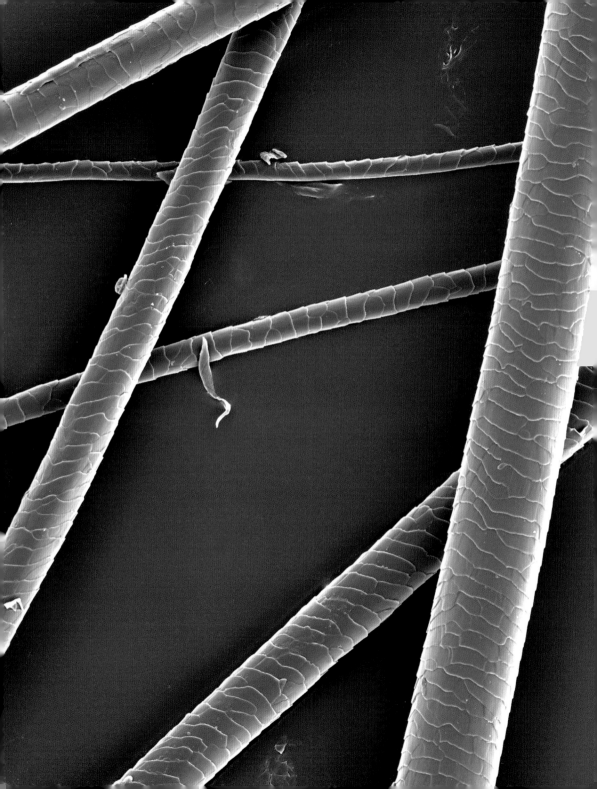

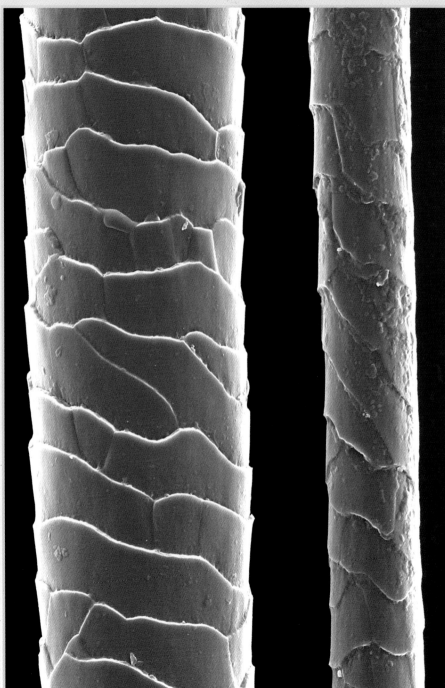

At a magnification of 750 times original size, the cuticle (outer surface) indicates the close overlapping that makes the hair so soft and resilient.

Opposite page: A magnified image of a Bichon Frise's hair magnified 200 times its original size.

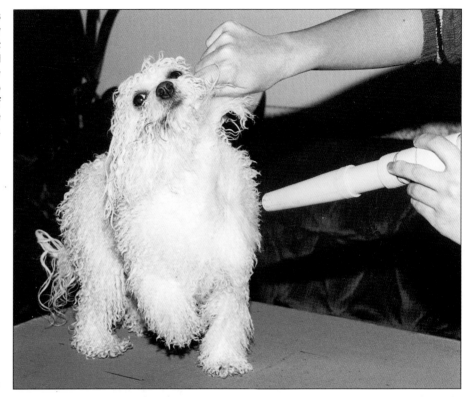

After the dog has been thoroughly toweled, the coat should be dried fully with a blow dryer. Be sure to aim the blast of air away from the dog's face.

to injure your dog, especially when working close to the eyes. The scissors must always be held flat on the coat when scissoring so as to achieve the desired effect.

Coat on the legs is scissored in a cylindrical fashion, not tapered in toward the foot. Also take care to hold the ears and mustache out of harm's way when scissoring the chest. Likewise, when scissoring the back end of the dog, make sure that the tail coat is moved so that it is not cut in error. Scissoring a Bichon properly is an art and takes a great

deal of practice, so new Bichon owners will need to take practical guidance from others who are more experienced.

Trimming below the pads of the feet prevents uncomfortable hairballs forming between the pads and enables the black pads of the feet to be seen. On males, most owners also trim off a little hair from the end of the penis, but a good half inch must be left so that tiny hairs do not aggravate the penis and set up infection. Also, whatever you do, take care not to cut through a nipple—and remember that males have little nipples too!

EAR CLEANING

On a Bichon, hair will also grow inside the ears. This should be carefully plucked out with blunt-ended tweezers. Remove only a few hairs at a time and this should be entirely painless. Ears must always be kept clean. This can be done using cotton balls. Many people use cotton swabs, but extreme care must be taken not to delve too deeply into the ears as this can cause injury. Be on the lookout for any signs of infection or ear-mite infestation. If your Bichon Frise has been shaking his head or scratching at his ears frequently, this usually indicates a problem. If his ears have an unusual odor, this is a sure sign of mite infestation or infection, and a signal to have his ears checked by the vet.

NAIL CLIPPING

Your Bichon Frise should be accustomed to having his nails trimmed at an early age, since it will be part of your maintenance routine throughout his life. Long nails are uncomfortable for any dog and can scratch someone unintentionally. Also, a long nail has a better chance of ripping and bleeding, or causing the feet to spread. A good rule of thumb is that if you can hear your dog's nails' clicking on the floor when he walks, his nails are too long.

Before you start cutting, make sure you can identify the "quick" in each nail. The quick is a blood vessel that runs through the center of each nail and grows rather close to the end. It will bleed if accidentally cut, which will be quite painful for the dog as it contains nerve endings. Keep some type of clotting agent on hand, such as a styptic pencil or styptic powder (the type used for shaving). This will stop the bleeding quickly when applied to the end of the cut nail. Do not panic if this happens, just stop the bleeding and talk soothingly to your dog. Once he has calmed down, move on to the next nail. It is better to clip a little at a time,

Be especially careful when scissoring your dog's face not to endanger the dog's eyes. The scissors must be held flat on the coat in order to achieve the desired round appearance.

Pet shops have special clippers made for cutting your dog's nails.

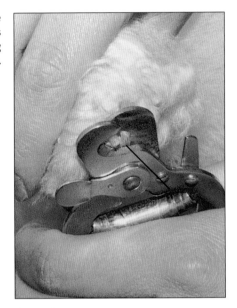

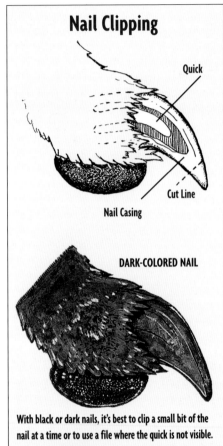

Nail Clipping

Quick

Cut Line

Nail Casing

DARK-COLORED NAIL

With black or dark nails, it's best to clip a small bit of the nail at a time or to use a file where the quick is not visible.

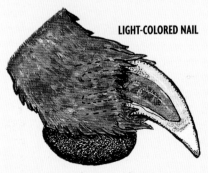

LIGHT-COLORED NAIL

In light-colored nails, clipping is much simpler because you can see the vein (or quick) that grows inside the casing.

particularly with black-nailed dogs like Bichons.

Hold your pup steady as you begin trimming his nails; you do not want him to make any sudden movements or run away. Talk to him soothingly and stroke him as you clip. Holding his foot in your hand, simply take off the end of each nail in one quick clip. You can purchase nail clippers that are specially made for dogs; you can find them wherever you buy grooming supplies.

TRAVELING WITH YOUR DOG

CAR TRAVEL
You should accustom your Bichon Frise to riding in a car at an early age. You may or may not take him in the car often, but at the very

The area around the nose and eyes is frequently dusted with a special powder to remove the stains, as evident on this just-bathed Bichon.

least he will need to go to the vet and you do not want these trips to be traumatic for the dog or a big hassle for you. The safest way for a dog to ride in the car is in his crate. If he uses a crate in the house, you can use the same crate for travel.

Put the pup in the crate and see how he reacts. If he seems uneasy, you can have a passenger hold him on his lap while you drive. Another option is a specially made safety harness for dogs, which straps the dog in much like a seat belt. Do not let the dog roam loose in the vehicle —this is very dangerous! If you should stop short, your dog can be thrown and injured. If the dog starts climbing on you and pestering you while you are driving, you will not be able to concentrate on the road. It is an unsafe

Your local pet shop will have a large supply of grooming tools that you can use on your Bichon.

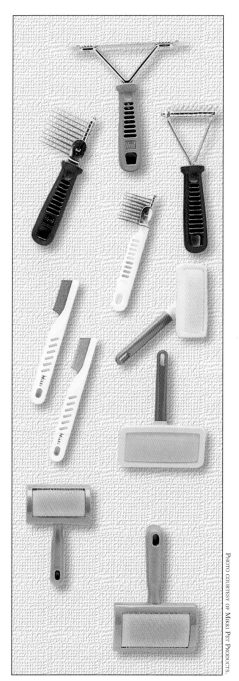

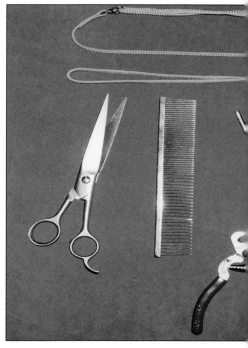

GROOMING EQUIPMENT

How much grooming equipment you purchase will depend on how much grooming you are going to do. Here are some basics:

- Natural bristle brush
- Slicker brush
- Metal comb
- Scissors
- Blow dryer
- Rubber mat
- Dog shampoo
- Spray hose attachment
- Ear cleaner
- Cotton balls
- Towels
- Nail clippers

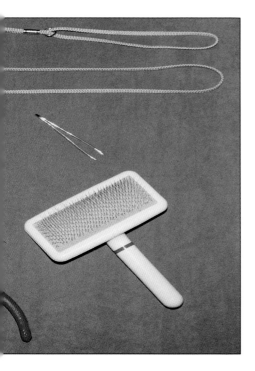

The safest method of car travel is by crate. Be sure your Bichons have proper ventilation while traveling.

(Center) These are the basic tools for grooming your Bichon Frise. Talk to a professional groomer to get more advice about and instruction in grooming.

situation for everyone—human and canine.

For long trips, be prepared to stop to let the dog relieve himself. Bring along whatever you need to clean up after him. You should take along some paper towels and perhaps some old rags for use should he have an accident in the car or suffer from motion sickness.

AIR TRAVEL

Contact your chosen airline before proceeding with your travel plans that include your Bichon Frise. The dog will be required to travel in a fiberglass crate and you should always check in advance

with the airline regarding specific requirements for the crate's size, type and labeling. To help put the dog at ease, give him one of his favorite toys in the crate. Do not feed the dog for several hours prior to checking in so that you minimize his need to relieve himself. However, some airlines require that the dog must be fed within four hours of arriving at the airport, in which case a light meal is best. For long trips, you will have to attach food and water bowls to the dog's crate so that airline employees can tend to him between legs of the trip.

ON THE ROAD

If you are going on a long motor trip with your dog, be sure the hotels are dog-friendly. Many hotels do not accept dogs. Also take along some ice that can be thawed and offered to your dog if he becomes overheated. Most dogs like to lick ice.

No matter how charming the photograph, each dog should have his own crate of the proper size.

BOARDING

So you want to take the family vacation—and you want to include *all* members of the family. Of course, you should make arrangements for accommodations ahead of time anyway, as this is especially important when traveling with a dog. You do not want to make an overnight stop at the only place around for miles and find out that they do not allow dogs. Also, you do not want to reserve a place for your family without confirming that you are traveling with a dog because if it is against their policy you may not have a place to stay.

Alternatively, if you are traveling and choose not to bring your Bichon Frise, you will have to make arrangements for him while you are away. Some options are to take him to a neighbor's house to stay while you are gone, to have a trusted neighbor stop by often or stay at your house, or bring your dog to a reputable boarding kennel or to your vet's office for boarding. If you choose to board him at a kennel, you should visit in advance to see the facility, how clean they are and where the dogs are kept. Talk to some of the employees and see how they treat the dogs—have they experience in grooming heavily coated dogs, do they spend time with the dogs, play with them, exercise them, etc.? Also find out the

TRAVELING ABROAD
For international travel you will have to make arrangements well in advance (perhaps months), as countries' regulations pertaining to bringing in animals differ. There may be special health certificates and/or vaccinations that your dog will need before taking the trip; sometimes this has to be done within a certain time frame. In rabies-free countries, you will need to bring proof of the dog's rabies vaccination and there may be a quarantine period upon arrival.

kennel's policy on vaccinations and what they require. This is for all of the dogs' safety, since when dogs are kept together, there is a greater risk of diseases being passed from dog to dog.

IDENTIFICATION

Your Bichon Frise is your valued companion and friend. That is why you always keep a close eye on him and you have made sure that he cannot escape from the yard or wriggle out of his collar and run away from you. However, accidents can happen and there may come a time when your dog unexpectedly gets separated from you. If this unfortunate event

should occur, the first thing on your mind will be finding him. Proper identification, including an ID tag, a tattoo and possibly a microchip, will increase the chances of his being returned to you safely and quickly.

You may find it necessary to board your dog on occasion. Your veterinarian can help you select a proper kennel, or you can visit the local kennels to find one with clean quarters, ample room for your dog and a knowledgeable caring staff that has experience with coated breeds.

IDENTIFICATION OPTIONS

As puppies become more and more expensive, especially those puppies of high quality for showing and/or breeding, they have a greater chance of being stolen. The usual collar dog tag is, of course, easily removed. But there are two more permanent techniques that have become widely used for identification.

The puppy microchip implantation involves the injection of a small microchip, about the size of a corn kernel, under the skin of the dog. If your dog shows up at a clinic or shelter, or is offered for resale under less-than-savory circumstances, it can be positively identified by the microchip. The microchip is scanned, and a registry quickly identifies you as the owner.

Tattooing is done on various parts of the dog, from his belly to his cheeks. The number tattooed can be your telephone number or any other number that you can easily memorize. When professional dog thieves see a tattooed dog, they usually lose interest. Both microchipping and tattooing can be done at your local veterinary clinic. For the safety of our dogs, no laboratory facility or dog broker will accept a tattooed dog as stock.

Discuss microchipping and tattooing with your veterinarian and breeder. Some vets perform these services on their own premises for a reasonable fee. Be certain that the dog do is then properly registered with a legitimate national database.

Training Your
BICHON FRISE

Living with an untrained dog is a lot like owning a piano that you do not know how to play—it is a nice object to look at but it does not do much more than that to bring you pleasure. Now try taking piano lessons and suddenly the piano comes alive and brings forth magical sounds and rhythms that set your heart singing and your body swaying.

The same is true with your Bichon. Any dog is a big responsibility and if not trained sensibly may develop unacceptable behavior that annoys you or could even cause

family friction.

To train your Bichon, you may like to enroll in an obedience class. Teach him good manners as you learn how and why he behaves the way he does. Find out how to communicate with your dog and how to recognize and understand his communications with you. Suddenly the dog takes on a new role in your life—he is smart, interesting, well behaved and fun to be with. He demonstrates his bond of devotion to you daily. In other words, your Bichon does wonders for your ego because he constantly reminds you that you are not only his leader, you are his hero!

Those involved with teaching dog obedience and counseling owners about their dogs' behavior have discovered some interesting facts about dog ownership. For example, training dogs when they are puppies results in the highest rate of success in developing well-mannered and well-adjusted adult dogs. Training an older dog, from six months to six years of age, can produce almost equal results, providing that the owner accepts the dog's slower rate of learning capability and is willing to work patiently to help the dog succeed at developing to his fullest poten-

REAP THE REWARDS

If you start with a normal, healthy dog and give him time, patience and some carefully executed lessons, you will reap the rewards of that training for the life of the dog. And what a life it will be! The two of you will find immeasurable pleasure in the companionship you have built together with love, respect and understanding.

It is up to you to select the relief area for your Bichon, else he may end up relieving himself in areas you'd rather he wouldn't.

tial. Unfortunately, many owners of untrained adult dogs lack the patience factor, so they do not persist until their dogs are successful at learning particular behaviors.

Training a puppy aged 10 to 16 weeks (20 weeks at the most) is like working with a dry sponge in a pool of water. The pup soaks up whatever you show him and constantly looks for more things to do and learn. At this early age, his body is not yet producing hormones, and therein lies the reason for such a high rate of success. Without hormones, he is focused on his owners and not particularly interested in investigating other places, dogs, people,

etc. You are his leader: his provider of food, water, shelter and security. He latches onto you and wants to stay close. He will usually follow you from room to room, will not let you out of his sight when you are outdoors with

PARENTAL GUIDANCE

Training a dog is a life experience. Many parents admit that much of what they know about raising children they learned from caring for their dogs. Dogs respond to love, fairness and guidance, just as children do. Become a good dog owner and you may become an even better parent.

Once the puppies begin producing hormones, their attention spans shrink. Training should begin immediately upon the new puppy's arrival to your home, when he is like a sponge ready to absorb a sea of new information.

him, and will respond in like manner to the people and animals you encounter. If you greet a friend warmly, he will be happy to greet the person as well. If, however, you are hesitant, even anxious, about the approach of a stranger, he will

CALM DOWN

Dogs will do anything for your attention. If you reward the dog when he is calm and resting, you will develop a well-mannered dog. If, on the other hand, you greet your dog excitedly and encourage him to wrestle with you, the dog will greet you the same way and you will have a hyperactive dog on your hands.

respond accordingly.

Once the puppy begins to produce hormones, his natural curiosity emerges and he begins to investigate the world around him. It is at this time when you may notice that the untrained dog begins to wander away from you and even ignore your commands to stay close. When this behavior becomes a problem, the owner has two choices: get rid of the dog or train him. It is strongly urged that you choose the latter option.

There are usually classes within a reasonable distance from the owner's home, but you also do a lot to train your dog yourself. Sometimes there are classes available but the tuition is too costly. Whatever the circumstances, the

THINK BEFORE YOU BARK

Dogs are sensitive to their masters' moods and emotions. Use your voice wisely when communicating with your dog. Never raise your voice at your dog unless you are trying to correct him. "Barking" at your dog can become as meaningless as "dogspeak" is to you.

solution to the problem of training your Bichon without formal obedience lessons lies within the pages of this book.

This chapter is devoted to helping you train your Bichon at home. If the recommended procedures are followed faithfully, you may expect positive results that will prove rewarding to both you and your dog.

Becoming house-trained is the minimum you should expect from your dog; he also must learn basic commands such as sit, heel, come and stay. Do not settle for anything less.

You should "train" yourself to clean up any canine deposits produced by your dog regardless of where they occur—inside or outside your yard.

Whether your new charge is a puppy or a mature adult, the methods of teaching and the techniques we use in training basic behaviors are the same. After all, no dog, whether puppy or adult, likes harsh or inhumane methods. All creatures, however, respond favorably to gentle motivational methods and sincere praise and encouragement. Now let us get started.

If you "program" your Bichon to relieve himself on grass, which is the most common choice of dog owners, then you must always bring him to this surface whenever you take him outside.

EXTRA! EXTRA!
Never line your pup's sleeping area with newspaper. Puppy litters are usually raised on newspaper and, once in your home, the puppy will immediately associate newspaper with voiding. Never put newspaper on any floor while house-training, as this will only confuse the puppy. If you are paper-training him, use paper in his designated relief area only. Finally, restrict water intake after evening meals. Offer a few licks at a time— never let a young puppy gulp water after meals.

HOUSEBREAKING
You can train a puppy to relieve himself wherever you choose, but this must be somewhere suitable. You should bear in mind from the outset that, when your puppy is old enough to go out in public places, any canine deposits must be removed at once. You will always have to carry with you a small plastic bag or "poop-scoop."

Outdoor training includes such surfaces as grass, dirt and cement. Indoor training usually means training your dog to newspaper. When deciding on the surface and location that you will want your Bichon to use, be sure it is going to be permanent. Training your dog to grass and then changing your mind two months later is extremely diffi-

CANINE DEVELOPMENT SCHEDULE

It is important to understand how and at what age a puppy develops into adulthood.
If you are a puppy owner, consult the following Canine Development Schedule to
determine the stage of development your puppy is currently experiencing.
This knowledge will help you as you work with the puppy in the weeks and months ahead.

Period	Age	Characteristics
FIRST TO THIRD	BIRTH TO SEVEN WEEKS	Puppy needs food, sleep and warmth, and responds to simple and gentle touching. Needs mother for security and disciplining. Needs littermates for learning and interacting with other dogs. Pup learns to function within a pack and learns pack order of dominance. Begin socializing pup with adults and children for short periods. Pup begins to become aware of his environment.
FOURTH	EIGHT TO TWELVE WEEKS	Brain is fully developed. Needs socializing with outside world. Remove from mother and littermates. Needs to change from canine pack to human pack. Human dominance necessary. Fear period occurs between 8 and 12 weeks. Avoid fright and pain.
FIFTH	THIRTEEN TO SIXTEEN WEEKS	Training and formal obedience should begin. Less association with other dogs, more with people, places, situations. Period will pass easily if you remember this is pup's change-to-adolescence time. Be firm and fair. Flight instinct prominent. Permissiveness and over-disciplining can do permanent damage. Praise for good behavior.
JUVENILE	FOUR TO EIGHT MONTHS	Another fear period about 7 to 8 months of age. It passes quickly, but be cautious of fright and pain. Sexual maturity reached. Dominant traits established. Dog should understand sit, down, come and stay by now.

NOTE: THESE ARE APPROXIMATE TIME FRAMES. ALLOW FOR INDIVIDUAL DIFFERENCES IN PUPPIES.

cult for both dog and owner.

Next, choose the command you will use each and every time you want your puppy to void. "Go hurry up" and "Potty" are examples of commands commonly used by dog owners.

Get in the habit of giving the puppy your chosen relief command before you take him out. That way, when he becomes an adult, you will be able to determine if he wants to go out when you ask him. A confirmation will

TAKE THE LEAD

Do not carry your dog to his relief area. Lead him there on a leash or, better yet, encourage him to follow you to the spot. If you start carrying him to his spot, you might end up doing this routine forever and your dog will have the satisfaction of having trained *you*.

be signs of interest, such as wagging his tail, watching you intently, going to the door, etc.

PUPPY'S NEEDS

The puppy needs to relieve himself after play periods, after each meal, after he has been sleeping and any time he indicates that he is looking for a place to urinate or defecate. The urinary and intestinal tract muscles of very young puppies are not fully developed. Therefore, like human babies, puppies need to relieve themselves frequently.

Take your puppy out often—every hour for an eight-week-old, for example, and always immediately after sleeping and eating. The older the puppy, the less often he will need to relieve himself. Finally, as a mature healthy adult, he will require only three to five relief trips per day.

HOUSING

Since the types of housing and control you provide for your puppy has a direct relationship on the success of house-training, we consider the various aspects of both before we begin training. Bringing a new puppy home and turning him loose in your house can be compared to turning a child loose in a sports arena and telling the child that the place is all his! The sheer enormity of the place would be too much for him to handle.

Instead, offer the puppy clearly defined areas where he can play, sleep, eat and live. A room of the house where the family gathers is the most obvious choice. Puppies are social animals and need to feel a part of the pack right from the start. Hearing your voice, watching you while you are doing things and smelling you nearby are all positive reinforcers that he is now a member of your pack. Usually a family room, the kitchen or a nearby adjoining breakfast area is ideal for providing safety and security for both puppy and owner.

Within that room there should be a smaller area that the puppy can call his own. An alcove, a wire or fiberglass dog crate or a fenced (not boarded!) corner from which he can view the activities of his new family will be fine. The size of the area or crate is the key factor here. The area must be large

A look that can melt a heart of steel! Puppies must relieve themselves on a regular basis, especially after meals, play periods and sleeping. This early training is very important. You want him to relieve himself in an area with which both of you are comfortable.

enough for the puppy to lie down and stretch out as well as stand up without rubbing his head on the top, yet small enough so that he cannot relieve himself at one end and sleep at the other without coming into contact with his droppings until fully trained to relieve himself outside.

The designated area should be lined with clean bedding and a toy. Water must always be available, in a non-spill container.

Dogs are, by nature, clean animals and will not remain close to their relief areas unless forced to do so. In those cases, they then become dirty dogs and usually remain that way for life.

HOW MANY TIMES A DAY?

AGE	RELIEF TRIPS
To 14 weeks	10
14–22 weeks	8
22–32 weeks	6
Adulthood	4
(dog stops growing)	

These are estimates, of course, but they are a guide to the *minimum* number of opportunities a dog should have each day to relieve himself.

CONTROL

By *control*, we mean helping the puppy to create a lifestyle pattern that will be compatible to that of his human pack (*you!*). Just as we guide little children to learn our way of life, we must show the puppy when it is time to play, eat, sleep, exercise and even entertain himself.

Your puppy should always sleep in his crate. He should also learn that, during times of household confusion and excessive human activity such as at breakfast when family members are preparing for the day, he can play by himself in relative safety and comfort in his designated area. Each time you leave the puppy alone, he should understand exactly where he is to stay. Puppies are chewers. They cannot tell the difference between chew toys and lamp cords, television wires, shoes, table legs, etc. Chewing into a television wire, for example, can be fatal to the puppy while a shorted wire can start a fire in the house.

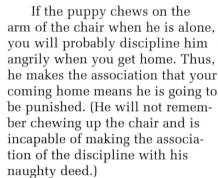

PLAN TO PLAY

The puppy should also have regular play and exercise sessions when he is with you or a family member. Exercise for a very young puppy can consist of a short walk around the house or yard. Playing can include fetching games with a large ball or a special toy. (All puppies teethe and need soft things upon which to chew.) Remember to restrict play periods to indoors within his living area (the family room, for example) until he is completely house-trained.

If the puppy chews on the arm of the chair when he is alone, you will probably discipline him angrily when you get home. Thus, he makes the association that your coming home means he is going to be punished. (He will not remember chewing up the chair and is incapable of making the association of the discipline with his naughty deed.)

Other times of excitement, such as friends' visits, family parties, etc., can be fun for the puppy providing he can view the activities from the security of his designated area. He is not underfoot and he is not being fed all sorts of tidbits that will probably cause him stomach distress, yet he still feels a part of the fun.

SCHEDULE

A puppy should be taken to his relief area each time he is released from his designated area, after meals, after a play session, when he first awakens in the morning (at age eight weeks, this can mean 5 a.m.!). The puppy will indicate that he's ready "to go" by circling or sniffing busily—do not misinterpret these signs. For a puppy less than ten weeks of age, a routine of taking him out every hour is necessary. As the puppy grows, he will be able to wait for longer periods of time.

Keep trips to his relief area short. Stay no more than five or six minutes and then return to the

You must determine how you want your Bichon Frise to behave. If you allow your dogs on the furniture, you may want to protect it with a cover or easily cleaned blanket.

house. If he goes during that time, praise him lavishly and take him indoors immediately. If he does not, but he has an accident when you go back indoors, pick him up immediately, say "No! No!" and return to his relief area. Wait a few minutes, then return to the house again. Never hit a puppy or put his face in urine or excrement when he has an accident!

Once indoors, put the puppy in his crate until you have had time to clean up his accident. Then release him to the family area and watch him more closely than before. Chances are, his accident was a result of your not pick-

ing up his signal or waiting too long before offering him the opportunity to relieve himself. Never hold a grudge against the puppy for accidents.

THE GOLDEN RULE

The golden rule of dog training is simple. For each "question" (command), there is only one correct answer (reaction). One command = one reaction. Keep practicing the command until the dog reacts correctly without hesitating. Be repetitive but not monotonous. Dogs get bored just as people do!

CONSISTENCY PAYS OFF

Dogs need consistency in their feeding schedule, exercise and relief visits, and in the verbal commands you use. If you use "Stay" on Monday and "Stay here, please" on Tuesday, you will confuse your dog. Don't demand perfect behavior during training sessions and then let him have the run of the house the rest of the day. Above all, lavish praise on your pet consistently every time he does something right. The more he feels he is pleasing you, the more willing he will be to learn.

for play versus the times for relief.

Help him develop regular hours for naps, being alone, playing by himself and just resting, all in his crate. Encourage him to entertain himself while you are busy with your activities. Let him learn that having you near is comforting, but it is not your main purpose in life to provide him with undivided attention. Each time you put a puppy in his own area, use the same command, whatever suits best. Soon, he will run to his crate or special area when he hears you say those words.

Crate training provides safety for you, the puppy and the home. It also provides the puppy with a feeling of security, and that helps the puppy achieve self-confidence and clean habits. Remember that one of the primary ingredients in house-training your puppy is control. Regardless of your lifestyle, there will always be occasions when you will need to have a place where your dog can stay and be happy and safe. Crate-training is the answer for now and in the future.

In conclusion, a few key elements are really all you need for a successful house-training method—consistency, frequency, praise, control and supervision. By following these procedures with a normal, healthy puppy, you and the puppy will soon be

Let the puppy learn that going outdoors means it is time to relieve himself, not play. Once trained, he will be able to play indoors and out and still differentiate between the times

past the stage of accidents and ready to move on to a clean and rewarding life together.

ROLES OF DISCIPLINE, REWARD AND PUNISHMENT

Discipline, training one to act in accordance with rules, brings order to life. It is as simple as that. Without discipline, particularly in a group society, chaos reigns supreme and the group will eventually perish. Humans and canines are social animals and need some form of discipline in order to function effectively. They

THE SUCCESS METHOD

Success that comes by luck is usually short-lived. Success that comes by well-thought-out proven methods is often more easily achieved and permanent. This is the Success Method. It is designed to give you, the puppy owner, a simple yet proven way to help your puppy develop clean living habits and a feeling of security in his new environment.

6 Steps to Successful Crate Training

1 Tell the puppy "Crate time!" and place him in the crate with a small treat (a piece of cheese or half of a biscuit). Let him stay in the crate for five minutes while you are in the same room. Then release him and praise lavishly. Never release him when he is fussing. Wait until he is quiet before you let him out.

2 Repeat Step 1 several times a day.

3 The next day, place the puppy in the crate as before. Let him stay there for ten minutes. Do this several times.

4 Continue building time in five-minute increments until the puppy stays in his crate for 30 minutes with you in the room. Always take him to his relief area after prolonged periods in his crate.

5 Now go back to Step 1 and let the puppy stay in his crate for five minutes, this time while you are out of the room.

6 Once again, build crate time in five-minute increments with you out of the room. When the puppy will stay willingly in his crate (he may even fall asleep!) for 30 minutes with you out of the room, he will be ready to stay in it for several hours at a time.

A wire crate offers your Bichon many advantages. In warmer climes, the wire crate is ideal for ventilation. Most Bichons like to be able to see what's going on about them.

must procure food, reproduce to keep the species going and protect their home base and their young. If there were no discipline in the lives of social animals, they would eventually die from starvation and/or predation by other stronger animals. In the case of domestic canines, dogs need discipline in their lives in order to understand how their pack (you and other family members) func-

THE CLEAN LIFE

By providing sleeping and resting quarters that fit the dog, and offering frequent opportunities to relieve himself outside his quarters, the puppy quickly learns that the outdoors (or the newspaper if you are training him to paper) is the place to go when he needs to urinate or defecate. It also reinforces his innate desire to keep his sleeping quarters clean. This, in turn, helps develop the muscle control that will eventually produce a dog with clean living habits.

tions and how they must act in order to survive.

A large humane society in a highly populated area recently surveyed dog owners regarding their satisfaction with their relationships with their dogs. People who had trained their dogs were 75% more satisfied with their pets than those who had never trained their dogs.

Dr. Edward Thorndike, a noted psychologist, established *Thorndike's Theory of Learning*, which states that a behavior that results in a pleasant event tends to be repeated. Likewise, a behavior that results in an unpleasant event tends not to be repeated. It is this theory on which training methods are based today. For example, if you manipulate a dog to perform a specific behavior and reward him for doing it, he is likely to do it again because he enjoyed the end result.

Occasionally, punishment, a penalty inflicted for an offense, is necessary. The best type of punishment often comes from an outside source. For example, a child is told not to touch the stove because he may get burned. He disobeys and touches the stove. In doing so, he receives a burn. From that time on, he respects the heat of the stove and avoids contact with it. Therefore, a behavior that results in an unpleasant event tends not to be repeated.

A good example of a dog

learning the hard way is the dog who chases the house cat. He is told many times to leave the cat alone, yet he persists in teasing the cat. Then, one day he begins chasing the cat but the cat turns and swipes a claw across the dog's face, leaving him with a painful gash on his nose. The final result is that the dog stops chasing the cat.

TRAINING EQUIPMENT

COLLAR AND LEASH
For a Bichon, the collar and leash that you use for training must be one with which you are easily able to work, not too heavy for the dog and perfectly safe.

TREATS
Have a bag of treats on hand. Something nutritious and easy to swallow works best. Use a soft treat, a chunk of cheese or a piece of cooked chicken rather than a dry biscuit. By the time the dog gets done chewing a dry treat, he will forget why he is being rewarded in the first place! Incidentally, using food rewards will not teach a dog to beg at the table—the only way to teach a dog to beg at the table is to give him food from the table. In training, rewarding the dog with a food treat will help him associate praise and the treats with learning new behaviors that obviously please his owner.

PRACTICE MAKES PERFECT!
- Have training lessons with your dog every day in several short segments—three to five times a day for a few minutes at a time is ideal.
- Do not have long practice sessions. The dog will become easily bored.
- Never practice when you are tired, ill, worried or in an otherwise negative mood. This will transmit to the dog and may have an adverse effect on his performance.

    Think fun, short and above all *positive*! End each session on a high note, rather than a failed exercise, and make sure to give a lot of praise. Enjoy the training and help your dog enjoy it, too.

TRAINING BEGINS: ASK THE DOG A QUESTION
In order to teach your dog anything, you must first get his attention. After all, he cannot learn anything if he is looking away from you with his mind on something else.

To get his attention, ask him "School?" and immediately walk over to him and give him a treat as you tell him "Good dog." Wait a minute or two and repeat the routine, this time with a treat in your hand as you approach within a foot of the dog. Do not go directly to him, but stop about a foot short of him and hold out the treat as you ask "School?" He will see you approaching with a treat

Dogs pay as much attention to your tone of voice and volume as they do to the words you use. The Bichon is especially sensitive to his owner's feelings and mood.

in your hand and most likely begin walking toward you. As you meet, give him the treat and praise again.

The third time, ask the question, have a treat in your hand and walk only a short distance toward the dog so that he must walk almost all the way to you. As he reaches you, give him the treat and praise again.

By this time, the dog will probably be getting the idea that if he pays attention to you, especially when you ask that question, it will pay off in treats and fun activities for him. In other words, he learns that "school" means doing fun things with you that

result in treats and positive attention for him.

Remember that the dog does not understand your verbal language, he only recognizes sounds. Your question translates to a series of sounds for him, and those sounds become the signal to go to you and pay attention; if he does, he will get to interact with you plus receive treats and praise.

THE BASIC COMMANDS

TEACHING SIT

Now that you have the dog's attention, attach his leash and hold it in your left hand and a food treat in your right. Place your food hand at the dog's nose and let him lick the treat but not take it from you. Say "Sit" and slowly raise your food hand from in front of the dog's nose up over his head so that he is looking at the ceiling. As he bends his head upward, he will have to bend his knees to maintain his balance. As he bends his knees, he will assume a sit

FAMILY TIES

If you have other pets in the home and/or interact often with the pets of friends and other family members, your pup will respond to those pets in much the same manner as you do. It is only when you show fear of or resentment toward another animal that he will act fearful or unfriendly.

FETCH!

Play fetching games with your puppy in an enclosed area where he can retrieve his toy and bring it back to you. Always use a toy or object designated just for this purpose. Never use a shoe, sock or other item he may later confuse with those in your closet or underneath your chair.

position. At that point, release the food treat and praise lavishly with comments such as "Good dog! Good sit!" Remember to always praise enthusiastically, because dogs relish verbal praise from their owners and feel so proud of themselves whenever they accomplish a behavior.

You will not use food forever in getting the dog to obey your commands. Food is only used to teach new behaviors, and once the dog knows what you want when you give a specific command, you

will wean him off the food treats but still maintain the verbal praise. After all, you will always have your voice with you, and there will be many times when you have no food rewards but expect the dog to obey.

TEACHING DOWN

Teaching the down exercise is easy when you understand how the dog perceives the down position, but it is very difficult when you do not. Dogs perceive the down position as a submissive one, therefore teaching the down exercise using a forceful method can sometimes make the dog develop such a fear of the down that he either runs away when you say "Down" or he attempts to snap at the person who tries to force him down.

Have the dog sit close alongside your left leg, facing in the same direction as you are. Hold the leash in your left hand and a food treat in your right. Now place your left hand lightly on the top of the dog's shoulders where they meet above the spinal cord. Do not push down on the dog's shoulders; simply rest your left hand there so you can guide the dog to lie down close to your left leg rather than to swing away from your side when he drops.

Now place the food hand at the dog's nose, say "Down" very softly (almost a whisper) and slowly lower the food hand to the

during the teaching process as we help the dog to understand exactly what it is that we are expecting him to do.

To teach the sit/stay, start with the dog sitting on your left side as before and hold the leash in your left hand. Have a food treat in your right hand and place your food hand at the dog's nose. Say "Stay" and step out on your right foot to stand directly in front of the dog, toe to toe, as he licks and nibbles the treat. Be sure to keep his head facing upward to maintain the sit position. Count to five and then swing around to stand next to the dog again with him on your left. As soon as you get back to the original position, release the food and praise lavishly.

To teach the down/stay, do the down as previously described. As soon as the dog lies down, say "Stay" and step out on your right foot just as you did in the sit/stay. Count to five and then return to stand beside the dog with him on your left side. Release the treat and praise as always.

Within a week or ten days, you can begin to add a bit of distance between you and your dog when you leave him. When you do, use your left hand open with the palm facing the dog as a stay signal, much the same as the hand signal a police officer uses to stop traffic at an intersection. Hold the food treat in your right hand as before, but this time the food is not touching

Do not try to teach the down exercise by forcing your dog into the down position. Instead, guide him gently while reassuring him and perhaps coaxing with a treat.

dog's front feet. When the food hand reaches the floor, begin moving it forward along the floor in front of the dog. Keep talking softly to the dog, saying things like, "Do you want this treat? You can do this, good dog." Your reassuring tone of voice will help calm the dog as he tries to follow the food hand in order to get the treat.

When the dog's elbows touch the floor, release the food and praise softly. Try to get the dog to maintain that down position for several seconds before you let him sit up again. The goal here is to get the dog to settle down and not feel threatened.

TEACHING STAY

It is easy to teach the dog to stay in either a sit or a down position. Again, we use food and praise

the dog's nose. He will watch the food hand and quickly learn that he is going to get that treat as soon as you return to his side.

When you can stand 1 yard away from your dog for 30 seconds, you can then begin building time and distance in both stays. Eventually, the dog can be expected to remain in the stay position for prolonged periods of time until you return to him or call him to you. Always praise lavishly when he stays.

TEACHING COME

If you make teaching "come" a fun experience, you should never have a student that does not love the game or that fails to come when called. The secret, it seems, is never to teach the word "come."

At times when an owner most wants his dog to come when called, the owner is likely upset or anxious and he allows these

Use your voice and hand signals to train your Bichon Frise to sit and stay. Have patience and be sure to retain eye contact when training your dog.

A food reward and a favorite toy are two good motivators to ensure that the dog will happily come to you.

treat as a reward for "winning."

A few turns of the "Where are you?" game and the dog will figure out that everyone is playing the game and that each person has a big celebration awaiting his success at locating him. Once the dog learns to love the game, simply calling out "Where are you?" will bring him running from wherever he is when he hears that all-important question.

The come command is recognized as one of the most important things to teach a dog, but there are trainers who work with thousands of dogs and never teach the actual word "come." Yet these dogs will race to respond to a person who uses the dog's name followed by "Where are you?" For example, a woman has a 12-year-old companion dog who went blind, but who never fails to locate her owner when asked, "Where are you?"

Children particularly love to

feelings to come through in the tone of his voice when he calls his dog. Hearing that desperation in his owner's voice, the dog fears the results of going to him and therefore either disobeys outright or runs in the opposite direction. The secret, therefore, is to teach the dog a game and, when you want him to come to you, simply play the game. It is practically a no-fail solution!

To begin, have several members of your family take a few food treats and each go into a different room in the house. Take turns calling the dog, and each person should celebrate the dog's finding him with a treat and lots of happy praise. When a person calls the dog, he is actually inviting the dog to find him and get a

"WHERE ARE YOU?"
When calling the dog, do not say "Come." Say things like, "Rover, where are you? See if you can find me! I have a biscuit for you!" Keep up a constant line of chatter with coaxing sounds and frequent questions such as, "Where are you?" The dog will learn to follow the sound of your voice to locate you and receive his reward.

play this game with their dogs. Children can hide in smaller places like a shower or bathtub, behind a bed or under a table. The dog needs to work a little bit harder to find these hiding places, but when he does he loves to celebrate with a treat and a tussle with a favorite youngster.

TEACHING HEEL

Heeling means that the dog walks beside the owner without pulling. It takes time and patience on the owner's part to succeed at teaching the dog that he (the owner) will not proceed unless the dog is walking calmly beside him. Pulling out ahead on the leash is definitely not acceptable.

Begin with holding the leash in your left hand as the dog sits beside your left leg. Move the loop end of the leash to your right hand but keep your left hand short on the leash so it keeps the dog in close next to you.

Say "Heel" and step forward on your left foot. Keep the dog close to you and take three steps. Stop and have the dog sit next to you in what we now call the heel position. Praise verbally, but do not touch the dog. Hesitate a moment and begin again with "Heel," taking three steps and stopping, at which point the dog is told to sit again.

Your goal here is to have the dog walk those three steps without pulling on the leash. When he

"COME" . . . BACK
Never call your dog to come to you for a correction or scold him when he reaches you. That is the quickest way to turn a "Come" command into "Go away fast!" Dogs think only in the present tense, and your dog will connect the scolding with coming to you, not with the misbehavior of a few moments earlier.

will walk calmly beside you for three steps without pulling, increase the number of steps you take to five. When he will walk politely beside you while you take five steps, you can increase the length of your walk to ten steps. Keep increasing the length of your stroll until the dog will walk quietly beside you without pulling as long as you want him to heel. When you stop heeling, indicate to the dog that the exercise is over by verbally praising as you pet him and say "OK, good dog." The "OK" is used as a release word, meaning that the exercise is finished and the dog is free to relax.

If you are dealing with a dog who insists on pulling you around, simply "put on your brakes" and stand your ground until the dog realizes that the two of you are not going anywhere until he is beside you and moving at your pace, not his. It may take some time just standing there to

Heeling means that the dog should walk alongside you exactly as shown in this photograph. The dog should neither be pulling on the leash ahead of you nor lagging behind.

TUG OF WALK?

If you begin teaching the heel by taking long walks and letting the dog pull you along, he misinterprets this action as an acceptable form of taking a walk. When you pull back on the lead to counteract his pulling, he reads that tug as a signal to pull even harder!

convince the dog that you are the leader and you will be the one to decide on the direction and speed of your travel.

Each time the dog looks up at you or slows down to give a slack leash between the two of you, quietly praise him and say, "Good heel. Good dog." Eventually, the dog will begin to respond and within a few days he will be walking politely beside you without pulling on the leash. At first, the training sessions should be kept short and very positive; soon the dog will be able to walk nicely with you for increasingly longer distances. Remember also to give the dog free time and the opportunity to run and play when you are done with heel practice.

WEANING OFF FOOD IN TRAINING

Food is used in training new behaviors. Once the dog understands what behavior goes with a specific command, it is time to start weaning him off the food

treats. At first, give a treat after each exercise. Then, start to give a treat only after every other exercise. Mix up the times when you offer a food reward and the times when you only offer praise so that the dog will never know when he is going to receive both food and praise and when he is going to receive only praise. This is called a variable ratio reward system and it proves successful because there is always the chance that the owner will produce a treat, so the dog never stops trying for that

reward. No matter what, *always* give verbal praise.

OBEDIENCE CLASSES

It is a good idea to enroll in an obedience class if one is available in your area. If yours is a show dog, handling classes would be more appropriate. Many areas have dog clubs that offer basic obedience training as well as preparatory classes for obedience competition. There are also local dog trainers who offer similar classes.

Agility competition is fun for dogs of all sizes. The easily trainable Bichon often excels in agility and has a lot of fun with it as well.

More than just a powder puff of loveliness, the Bichon Frise is trainable and obedient.

At obedience trials, dogs can earn titles at various levels of competition. The beginning levels of competition include basic behaviors such as sit, down, heel, etc. The more advanced levels of competition include jumping, retrieving, scent discrimination and signal work. The advanced levels require a dog and owner to put a lot of time and effort into their training and the titles that can be earned at these levels of competition are very prestigious.

OTHER ACTIVITIES FOR LIFE

Whether a dog is trained in the structured environment of a class or alone with his owner at home, there are many activities that can bring fun and rewards to both owner and dog once they have mastered basic control.

Teaching the dog to help out around the home, in the yard or on the farm provides great satisfaction to both dog and owner. In addition, the dog's help makes life a little easier for his owner and raises his stature as a valued companion to his family. It helps give the dog a purpose by occupying his mind and providing an outlet for his energy.

Hiking is an exciting and healthy activity that the dog can be taught without assistance from more than his owner. The exercise of walking and climbing is good for man and dog alike,

and the bond that they develop together is priceless.

If you are interested in participating in organized competition with your Bichon, there are activities other than obedience in which you and your dog can become involved. Agility is a popular and fun sport where dogs run through an obstacle course that includes various jumps, tunnels and other exercises to test the dog's speed and coordination. The owners run through the course beside their dogs to give commands and to guide them through the course. Although competitive, the focus is on fun—it's fun to do, fun to watch and great exercise.

Walking on the beach, jogging and hiking are all within the realm of possibility with your adult Bichon.

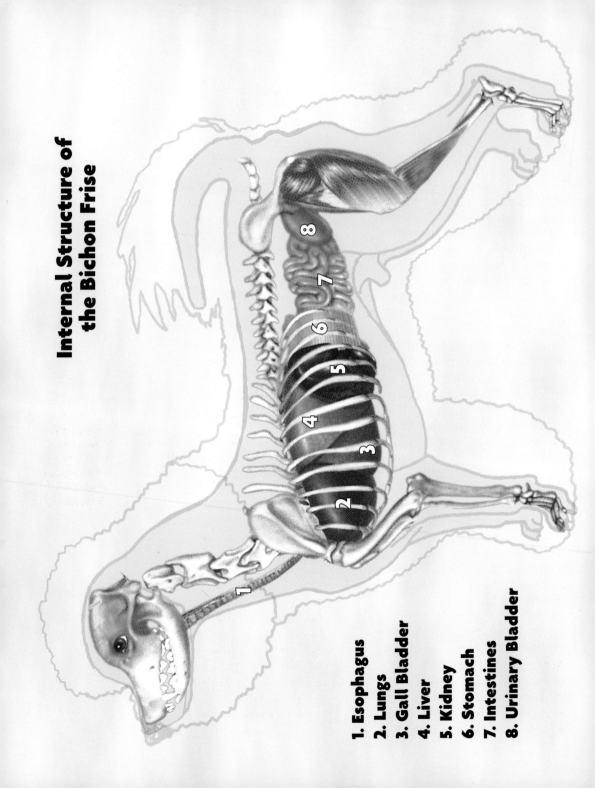

Internal Structure of the Bichon Frise

1. Esophagus
2. Lungs
3. Gall Bladder
4. Liver
5. Kidney
6. Stomach
7. Intestines
8. Urinary Bladder

BICHON FRISE

Dogs suffer from many of the same physical illnesses as people. They might even share many of the same psychological problems. Since people usually know more about human diseases than canine maladies, many of the terms used in this chapter will be familiar but not necessarily those used by veterinarians. We will use the term *x-ray*, instead of the more acceptable term *radiograph*. We will also use the familiar term *symptom*. Even though dogs don't have symptoms, which are verbal descriptions of the patient's feelings, dogs have *clinical signs*. Since dogs can't speak, we have to look for clinical signs...but we still use the term *symptom* in this book.

As a general rule, medicine is *practiced*. That term is not arbitrary. Medicine is a constantly changing art as we learn more and more about genetics, electronic aids (like CAT scans and MRIs) and daily laboratory advances.

There are many dog maladies, like canine hip dysplasia, which are not universally treated in the same manner. Some veterinarians opt for surgery more often than others do.

SELECTING A QUALIFIED VET
Your selection of a veterinarian should be based not only upon personality and ability with coated dogs but also upon his convenience to your home. You want a vet who is close because you might have emergencies or need to make multiple visits for treatments. You want a vet who has services that you might require such as a boarding kennel and grooming facilities, as well as pet supplies and a good reputation for ability and responsiveness. There is nothing more frustrating than having to wait a day or more to get a response from your veterinarian.

All veterinarians are licensed and their diplomas and/or certifi-

The veterinarian of choice is knowledgeable about Bichons, conversant with modern veterinary techniques and close to your home.

Breakdown of Veterinary Income by Category

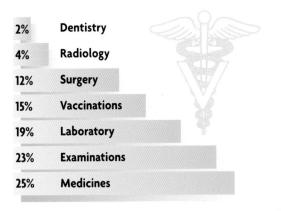

2%	Dentistry
4%	Radiology
12%	Surgery
15%	Vaccinations
19%	Laboratory
23%	Examinations
25%	Medicines

A typical vet's income, categorized according to services performed. This survey dealt with small-animal (pet) practices.

cates should be displayed in their waiting rooms. There are, however, many veterinary specialties that usually require further studies and internships. There are specialists in heart problems (veterinary cardiologists), skin problems (veterinary dermatologists), teeth and gum problems (veterinary dentists), eye problems (veterinary ophthalmologists), x-rays (veterinary radiologists), and vets who have specialties in bones, muscles or certain organs. Most veterinarians do routine surgery such as neutering, stitching up wounds and docking tails for those breeds in which such is required for show purposes. When the problem affecting your dog is serious, it is not unusual or impudent to get another medical opinion, although it is courteous to advise the vets concerned about this. You might also want to

compare costs among several veterinarians. Sophisticated health care and veterinary services can be very costly. Don't be bashful about discussing these costs with your veterinarian or his staff. It is not infrequent that important decisions are based upon financial considerations.

PREVENTATIVE MEDICINE

It is much easier, less costly and more effective to practice preventative medicine than to fight bouts of illness and disease. Properly bred puppies come from parents that were selected based upon their genetic-disease profile. Their mother should have been vaccinated, free of all internal and external parasites and properly nourished. For these reasons, a visit to the veterinarian who cared for the dam is recommended. The dam can pass on disease resistance to her puppies, which can last for eight to ten weeks. She can also pass on parasites and many infections. That's why you should learn as much about the dam's health as possible.

WEANING TO FIVE MONTHS OLD

Puppies should be weaned by the time they are about two months old. A puppy that remains for at least eight weeks with his mother and littermates usually adapts better to other dogs and people later in his life.

First Aid at a Glance

Burns
Place the affected area under cool water; use ice if only a small area is burnt.

Bee stings/Insect bites
Apply ice to relieve swelling; antihistamine dosed properly.

Animal bites
Clean any bleeding area; apply pressure until bleeding subsides; go to the vet.

Spider bites
Use cold compress and a pressurized pack to inhibit venom's spreading.

Antifreeze poisoning
Immediately induce vomiting by using hydrogen peroxide.

Fish hooks
Removal best handled by vet; hook must be cut in order to remove.

Snake bites
Pack ice around bite; contact vet quickly; identify snake for proper antivenin.

Car accident
Move dog from roadway with blanket; seek veterinary aid.

Shock
Calm the dog, keep him warm; seek immediate veterinary help.

Nosebleed
Apply cold compress to the nose; apply pressure to any visible abrasion.

Bleeding
Apply pressure above the area; treat wound by applying a cotton pack.

Heat stroke
Submerge dog in cold bath; cool down with fresh air and water; go to the vet.

Frostbite/Hypothermia
Warm the dog with a warm bath, electric blankets or hot water bottles.

Abrasions
Clean the wound and wash out thoroughly with fresh water; apply antiseptic.

 Remember: an injured dog may attempt to bite a helping hand from fear and confusion. Always muzzle the dog before trying to offer assistance.

Some new owners have their puppy examined by a veterinarian immediately, which is a good idea. The puppy will have his teeth examined and have his skeletal conformation and general health checked prior to certification by the veterinarian. Puppies in certain breeds have problems with their kneecaps, cataracts and other eye problems, heart murmurs and undescended testicles. They may also have personality problems and your veterinarian might have training in temperament evaluation.

VACCINATION SCHEDULING
Vaccination programs usually begin when the puppy is very young. Most vaccinations are given by injection and should

DEWORMING PUPPY
Caring for the puppy starts before the puppy is born by keeping the dam healthy and well-nourished. Most puppies have worms, even if they are not evident, so a worming program is essential. The worms continually shed eggs except during their dormant stage, when they just rest in the tissues of the puppy. During this stage they are not evident during a routine examination.

only be done by a veterinarian. Both he and you should keep a record of the date of the injection, the identification of the vaccine and the amount given. Some vets give a first vaccination at eight weeks, but most dog breeders prefer the course not to commence until about ten weeks because of negating any antibodies passed on by the dam. The vaccination scheduling is usually based on a 15-day cycle. You must take your vet's advice as to when to vaccinate as this may differ according to the vaccine used. Most vaccinations immunize your puppy against viruses.

The usual vaccines contain immunizing doses of several different viruses such as distemper, parvovirus, parainfluenza and hepatitis. There are other vaccines available when the puppy is at risk. You should rely upon professional advice. This is especially true for the booster-shot program. Most vaccination programs require a booster when the puppy is a year old and once a year thereafter. In some cases, circumstances may require more frequent immunizations. Canine cough, more formally known as tracheobronchitis, is treated with a vaccine that is sprayed into the dog's nostrils. Canine cough is usually included in routine vaccination, but this is often not so effective as for other major diseases.

Normal Skeletal Structure of the Bichon Frise

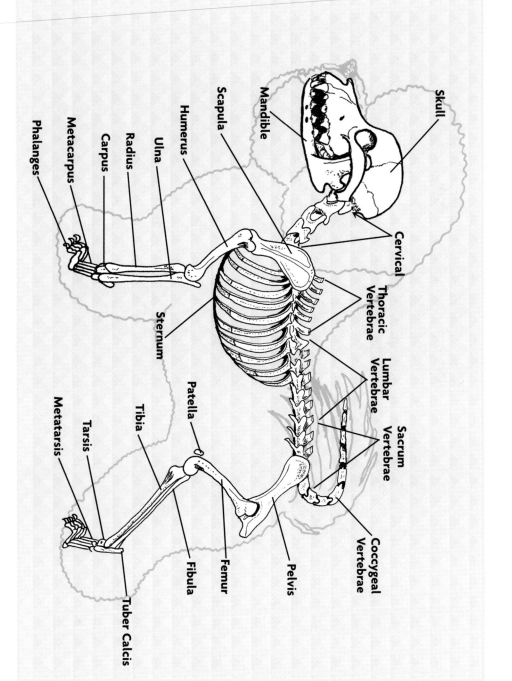

Skull

Cervical

Thoracic Vertebrae

Lumbar Vertebrae

Sacrum Vertebrae

Coccygeal Vertebrae

Pelvis

Femur

Fibula

Patella

Tibia

Tarsis

Metatarsis

Tuber Calcis

Phalanges

Metacarpus

Carpus

Radius

Ulna

Humerus

Scapula

Mandible

Sternum

HEALTH AND VACCINATION SCHEDULE

Age in Weeks:	6TH	8TH	10TH	12TH	14TH	16TH	20-24TH	52ND
Worm Control	✔	✔	✔	✔	✔	✔	✔	
Neutering								✔
Heartworm		✔		✔		✔	✔	
Parvovirus	✔		✔		✔		✔	✔
Distemper		✔		✔		✔		✔
Hepatitis		✔		✔		✔		✔
Leptospirosis								✔
Parainfluenza	✔		✔		✔			✔
Dental Examination		✔					✔	✔
Complete Physical		✔					✔	✔
Coronavirus				✔			✔	✔
Canine Cough	✔							
Hip Dysplasia								✔
Rabies							✔	

Vaccinations are not instantly effective. It takes about two weeks for the dog's immune system to develop antibodies. Most vaccinations require annual booster shots. Your vet should guide you in this regard.

FIVE MONTHS TO ONE YEAR OF AGE
Unless you intend to breed or show your dog, neutering the puppy at six months of age is recommended. Discuss this with your veterinarian; most professionals advise neutering the puppy. Neutering and spaying are routine procedures, and the best option for pet dogs of both sexes. Neutering has proven to be extremely beneficial to both male and female dogs. Besides eliminating the possibility of pregnancy, it inhibits (but does not prevent) breast cancer in bitches and prostate cancer in male dogs. Under no circumstances should a bitch be spayed prior to her first season.

DOGS OLDER THAN ONE YEAR
Continue to visit the vet at least once a year. There is no such disease as old age, but bodily functions do change with age. The eyes and ears are no longer as efficient. Liver, kidney and intestinal functions often decline. Proper dietary changes can make life more pleasant for the aging Bichon Frise and you.

SKIN PROBLEMS IN BICHONS FRISES

Veterinarians are consulted by dog owners for skin problems more than any other group of diseases or maladies. Dogs' skin is almost as sensitive as human skin and both suffer almost the same ailments (though the occurrence of acne in dogs is rare!). For this reason, veterinary dermatology has developed into a specialty practiced by many vets.

Since many skin problems have visual symptoms that are almost identical, it requires the skill of an experienced veterinary dermatologist to identify and cure many of the more severe skin disorders. Pet shops sell many treatments for skin problems but most of the treatments are directed at symptoms and not the underlying problem(s). If your dog is suffering from a skin disorder, you should seek professional assistance as quickly as possible. As with all diseases, the earlier a problem is identified and treated, the more likely is the cure.

DISEASE REFERENCE CHART

	What is it?	What causes it?	Symptoms
Leptospirosis	Severe disease that affects the internal organs; can be spread to people.	A bacterium, which is often carried by rodents, that enters through mucous membranes and spreads quickly throughout the body.	Range from fever, vomiting and loss of appetite in less severe cases to shock, irreversible kidney damage and possibly death in most severe cases.
Rabies	Potentially deadly virus that infects warm-blooded mammals.	Bite from a carrier of the virus, mainly wild animals.	1st stage: dog exhibits change in behavior, fear. 2nd stage: dog's behavior becomes more aggressive. 3rd stage: loss of coordination, trouble with bodily functions.
Parvovirus	Highly contagious virus, potentially deadly.	Ingestion of the virus, which is usually spread through the feces of infected dogs.	Most common: severe diarrhea. Also vomiting, fatigue, lack of appetite.
Canine cough	Contagious respiratory infection.	Combination of types of bacteria and virus. Most common: *Bordetella bronchiseptica* bacteria and parainfluenza virus.	Chronic cough.
Distemper	Disease primarily affecting respiratory and nervous system.	Virus that is related to the human measles virus.	Mild symptoms such as fever, lack of appetite and mucous secretion progress to evidence of brain damage, "hard pad."
Hepatitis	Virus primarily affecting the liver.	Canine adenovirus type I (CAV-1). Enters system when dog breathes in particles.	Lesser symptoms include listlessness, diarrhea, vomiting. More severe symptoms include "blue-eye" (clumps of virus in eye).
Coronavirus	Virus resulting in digestive problems.	Virus is spread through infected dog's feces.	Stomach upset evidenced by lack of appetite, vomiting, diarrhea.

HEREDITARY SKIN DISORDERS

Veterinary dermatologists are currently researching a number of skin disorders that are believed to have a hereditary basis. These inherited diseases are transmitted by both parents, who appear (phenotypically) normal but have a recessive gene for the disease, meaning that they carry, but are not affected by, the disease. These diseases pose serious problems to breeders because in some instances there are no methods of identifying carriers. Often the secondary diseases associated with these skin conditions are even more debilitating than the skin disorders themselves, including cancers and respiratory problems.

Among the hereditary skin disorders, for which the mode of inheritance is known, are acrodermatitis, cutaneous asthenia (Ehlers-Danlos syndrome), sebaceous adenitis, cyclic hematopoiesis, dermatomyositis, IgA deficiency, color dilution alopecia and nodular dermatofibrosis. Some of these disorders are limited to one or two breeds, while others affect a large number of breeds. All inherited diseases must be diagnosed and treated by a veterinary specialist.

PARASITE BITES

Many of us are allergic to insect bites. The bites itch, erupt and may even become infected. Dogs have the same reaction to fleas,

DENTAL HEALTH

A dental examination is in order when the dog is between six months and one year of age so that any permanent teeth that have erupted incorrectly can be corrected. It is important to begin a brushing routine, preferably using a two-sided brushing technique, whereby both sides of the tooth are brushed at the same time. Durable nylon and safe edible chews should be a part of your puppy's arsenal for good health, good teeth and pleasant breath. The vast majority of dogs three to four years old and older has diseases of the gums from lack of dental attention. Using the various types of dental chews can be very effective in controlling dental plaque.

ticks and/or mites. When an insect lands on you, you have the chance to whisk it away with your hand. Unfortunately, when your dog is bitten by a flea, tick or mite, he can only scratch it away or bite it. By the time the dog has been bitten, the parasite has done some of its damage. It may also have laid eggs to cause further problems in the near future. The itching from parasite bites is probably due to the saliva injected into the site when the parasite sucks the dog's blood.

AUTO-IMMUNE SKIN CONDITIONS

Auto-immune skin conditions are commonly referred to as being allergic to yourself, while allergies are usually inflammatory reactions to an outside stimulus. Auto-immune diseases cause serious damage to the tissues that are involved.

The best known auto-immune disease is lupus, which affects people as well as dogs. The symptoms are variable and may affect the kidneys, bones, blood chemistry and skin. It can be fatal to both dogs and humans, though it is not thought to be transmissible. It is usually successfully treated with cortisone, prednisone or similar corticosteroid, but extensive use of these drugs can have harmful side effects.

Many parasites and allergens can harbor in the grass. Keep this in mind whenever your snowy-coated Bichon visits the great outdoors.

AIRBORNE ALLERGIES

Just as humans have hay fever, rose fever and other fevers from which they suffer during the pollinating season, many dogs suffer from the same allergies. When the pollen count is high, your dog might suffer but don't expect them

Be on your toes to keep your Bichon smiling.

KNOW WHEN TO POSTPONE A VACCINATION

While the visit to the vet is costly, it is never advisable to update a vaccination when visiting with a sick or pregnant dog. Vaccinations should be avoided for all elderly dogs. If your dog is showing the signs of any illness or any medical condition, no matter how serious or mild, including skin irritations, do not vaccinate. Likewise, a lame dog should never be vaccinated; any dog undergoing surgery or on any immunosuppressant drugs should not be vaccinated until fully recovered.

to sneeze and have runny noses as a human would. Dogs react to pollen allergies the same way they react to fleas—they scratch and bite themselves. Dogs, like humans, can be tested for allergens. Discuss the testing with your veterinary dermatologist.

FOOD PROBLEMS

FOOD ALLERGIES

Dogs can be allergic to many foods that are best-sellers and highly recommended by breeders and veterinarians. Changing the brand of food that you buy may not eliminate the problem if the element to which the dog is allergic is contained in the new brand.

Recognizing a food allergy is difficult. Humans vomit or have rashes when we eat a food to which we are allergic. Dogs neither vomit nor (usually) develop a rash. They react in the same manner as they do to an airborne or flea allergy: they itch, scratch and bite. Thus making the diagnosis extremely difficult. While pollen allergies and parasite bites are usually seasonal, food allergies are year-round problems.

FOOD INTOLERANCE

Food intolerance is the inability of the dog to completely digest certain foods. For example, puppies that may have done very well on their mother's milk may not do well on cow's milk. The result of this food intolerance may be loose bowels, passing gas and stomach pains. These are the only obvious symptoms of food intolerance and that makes diagnosis difficult.

TREATING FOOD PROBLEMS

It is possible to handle food allergies and food intolerance yourself. Put your dog on a diet that he has never had. Obviously if he has never eaten this new food, he can't have been allergic or intolerant of it. Start with a single ingredient that is not in the dog's diet at the present time. Ingredients like chopped beef or chicken are common in dog's diets, so try something more exotic like rabbit, fish or another source of quality protein. Keep the dog on this diet (with no additives) for a month. If the symptoms of food allergy or intolerance disappear, chances are your dog has a food allergy.

Don't think that the single ingredient cured the problem. You still must find a suitable diet and ascertain which ingredient in the old diet was objectionable. This is most easily done by adding ingredients to the new diet one at a time. Let the dog stay on the modified diet for a month before you add another ingredient. Eventually, you will determine the ingredient that caused the adverse reaction.

An alternative method is to carefully study the ingredients in the diet to which your dog is allergic or intolerable. Identify the main ingredient in this diet and eliminate the main ingredient by buying a different food that does not have that ingredient. Keep experimenting until the symptoms disappear after one month on the new diet.

FAT OR FICTION?

The myth that dogs need extra fat in their diets can be harmful. Should your vet recommend extra fat, use safflower oil instead of animal oils. Safflower oil has been shown to be less likely to cause allergic reactions.

A male dog flea, *Ctenocephalides canis.*

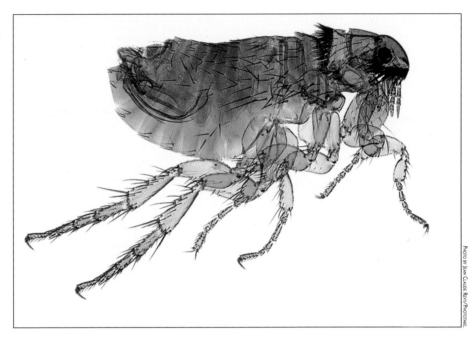

EXTERNAL PARASITES

FLEAS

Of all the problems to which dogs are prone, none is more well known and frustrating than fleas. Flea infestation is relatively simple to cure but difficult to prevent. Parasites that are harbored inside the body are a bit more difficult to eradicate but they are easier to control.

To control flea infestation, you have to understand the flea's life cycle. Fleas are often thought of as a summertime problem, but centrally heated homes have changed the patterns and fleas can be found at any time of the year. The most effective method of flea control is a two-stage approach: one stage to kill the adult fleas, and the other to control the development of pre-adult fleas. Unfortunately, no single active ingredient is effective against all stages of the life cycle.

FLEA KILLER CAUTION— "POISON"

Flea-killers are poisonous. You should not spray these toxic chemicals on areas of a dog's body that he licks, including his genitals and his face. Flea killers taken internally are a better answer, but check with your vet in case internal therapy is not advised for your dog.

LIFE CYCLE STAGES

During its life, a flea will pass through four life stages: egg, larva, pupa or nymph and adult. The adult stage is the most visible and irritating stage of the flea life cycle, and this is why the majority of flea-control products concentrate on this stage. The fact is that adult fleas account for only 1% of the total flea population, and the other 99% exist in pre-adult stages, i.e., eggs, larvae and nymphs. The pre-adult stages are barely visible to the naked eye.

THE LIFE CYCLE OF THE FLEA

Eggs are laid on the dog, usually in quantities of about 20 or 30, several times a day. The adult female flea must have a blood meal before each egg-laying session. When first laid, the eggs will cling to the dog's hair, as the eggs are still moist. However, they will quickly dry out and fall from the dog, especially if the dog moves around or scratches. Many eggs will fall off in the dog's favorite area or an area in which he spends a lot of time, such as his bed.

Once the eggs fall from the dog onto the carpet or furniture, they will hatch into larvae. This takes from one to ten days. Larvae are not particularly mobile and will usually travel only a few inches from where they hatch. However, they do have a tendency to move away from bright light and heavy

EN GARDE:
CATCHING FLEAS OFF GUARD!
Consider the following ways to arm yourself against fleas:
• Add a small amount of pennyroyal or eucalyptus oil to your dog's bath. These natural remedies repel fleas.
• Supplement your dog's food with fresh garlic (minced or grated) and a hearty amount of brewer's yeast, both of which ward off fleas.
• Use a flea comb on your dog daily. Submerge fleas in a cup of bleach to kill them quickly.
• Confine the dog to only a few rooms to limit the spread of fleas in the home.
• Vacuum daily...and get all of the crevices! Dispose of the bag every few days until the problem is under control.
• Wash your dog's bedding daily. Cover cushions where your dog sleeps with towels, and wash the towels often.

traffic—under furniture and behind doors are common places to find high quantities of flea larvae.

The flea larvae feed on dead organic matter, including adult flea feces, until they are ready to change into adult fleas. Fleas will usually remain as larvae for around seven days. After this period, the larvae will pupate into protective pupae. While inside the pupae, the larvae will undergo

Fleas have been measured as being able to jump 300,000 times and can jump 150 times their length in any direction, including straight up.

metamorphosis and change into adult fleas. This can take as little time as a few days, but the adult fleas can remain inside the pupae waiting to hatch for up to two years. The pupae are signaled to hatch by certain stimuli, such as physical pressure—the pupae's being stepped on, heat from an animal's lying on the pupae or increased carbon-dioxide levels and vibrations—indicating that a suitable host is available.

Once hatched, the adult flea must feed within a few days. Once the adult flea finds a host, it will not leave voluntarily. It only becomes dislodged by grooming or the host animal's scratching.

The adult flea will remain on the host for the duration of its life unless forcibly removed.

TREATING THE ENVIRONMENT AND THE DOG

Treating fleas should be a two-pronged attack. First, the environment needs to be treated; this includes carpets and furniture, especially the dog's bedding and areas underneath furniture. The environment should be treated with a household spray containing an Insect Growth Regulator (IGR) and an insecticide to kill the adult fleas. Most IGRs are effective against eggs and larvae; they actually mimic the fleas' own hormones and stop the eggs and larvae from developing into adult fleas. There are currently no treatments available to attack the pupa stage of the life cycle, so the adult insecticide is used to kill the newly hatched adult fleas before they find a host. Most IGRs are active for many months, while

A scanning electron micrograph of a dog or cat flea, *Ctenocephalides*, magnified more than 100x. This image has been colorized for effect.

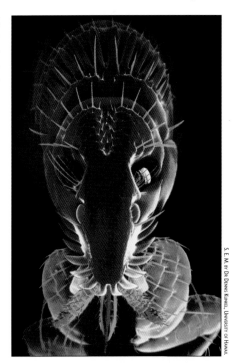

THE LIFE CYCLE OF THE FLEA

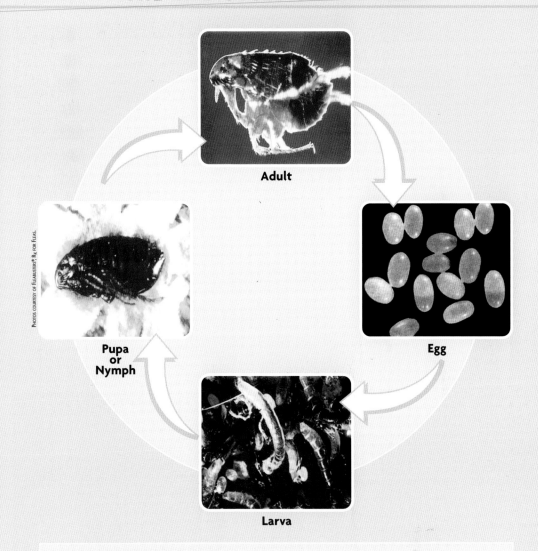

Adult

Egg

Larva

Pupa or Nymph

PHOTOS COURTESY OF FLEABUSTERS® Rx FOR FLEAS.

Fleas have been around for millions of years and have adapted to changing host animals. They are able to go through a complete life cycle in less than one month or they can extend their lives to almost two years by remaining as pupae or cocoons. They do not need blood or any other food for up to 20 months.

INSECT GROWTH REGULATOR (IGR)

Two types of products should be used when treating fleas—a product to treat the pet and a product to treat the home. Adult fleas represent less than 1% of the flea population. The pre-adult fleas (eggs, larvae and pupae) represent more than 99% of the flea population and are found in the environment; it is in the case of pre-adult fleas that products containing an Insect Growth Regulator (IGR) should be used in the home.

IGRs are a new class of compounds used to prevent the development of insects. They do not kill the insect outright, but instead use the insect's biology against it to stop it from completing its growth. Products that contain methoprene are the world's first and leading IGRs. Used to control fleas and other insects, this type of IGR will stop flea larvae from developing and protect the house for up to seven months.

adult insecticides are only active for a few days.

When treating with a household spray, it is a good idea to vacuum before applying the product. This stimulates as many pupae as possible to hatch into adult fleas. The vacuum cleaner should also be treated with an insecticide to prevent the eggs and larvae that have been collected in the vacuum bag from hatching.

The second stage of treatment is to apply an adult insecticide to the dog. Traditionally, this would be in the form of a collar or a spray, but more recent innovations include digestible insecticides that poison the fleas when they ingest the dog's blood. Alternatively, there are drops that, when placed on the back of the dog's neck, spread throughout the hair and skin to kill adult fleas.

TICKS

Though not as common as fleas, ticks are found all over the tropical and temperate world. They don't bite, like fleas; they harpoon. They dig their sharp proboscis (nose) into the dog's skin and drink the blood. Their

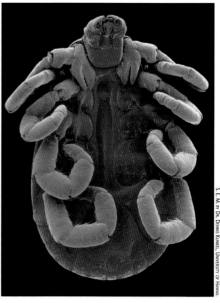

S.E.M. BY DR. DENNIS KUNKEL, UNIVERSITY OF HAWAII

only food and drink is dog's blood. Dogs can get Lyme disease, Rocky Mountain spotted fever, tick bite paralysis and many other diseases from ticks. They may live where fleas are found and they like to hide in cracks or seams in walls. They are controlled the same way fleas are controlled.

The American dog tick, *Dermacentor variabilis*, may well be the most common dog tick in many geographical areas, especially those areas where the climate is hot and humid. Most dog ticks have life expectancies of a week to six months, depending upon climatic conditions. They can neither jump nor fly, but they can crawl slowly and can range up to 16 feet to reach a sleeping or unsuspecting dog.

MITES
Just as fleas and ticks can be problematic for your dog, mites can also lead to an itchy nuisance. Microscopic in size, mites are related to ticks and generally take up permanent residence on their host animal—in this case, your dog! The term *mange* refers to any infestation caused by one of the mighty mites, of which there are six varieties that concern dog owners.

Demodex mites cause a condition known as demodicosis

DEER-TICK CROSSING
The great outdoors may be fun for your dog, but it also is an home to dangerous ticks. Deer ticks carry a bacterium known as *Borrelia burgdorferi* and are most active in the autumn and spring. When infections are caught early, penicillin and tetracycline are effective antibiotics, but if left untreated the bacteria may cause neurological, kidney and cardiac problems as well as long-term trouble with walking and painful joints.

S.E.M. BY DR. ANDREW SPIELMAN/PHOTOTAKE

PHOTO BY DR. DENNIS KUNKEL, UNIVERSITY OF HAWAII.

The head of an American dog tick, *Dermacentor variabilis,* enlarged and colorized for effect.

PHOTO BY JAMES HAYDEN/YOAV/PHOTOTAKE.

Human lice look
like dog lice;
the two are
closely related.
PHOTO BY DWIGHT R. KUHN.

(sometimes called red mange or follicular mange), in which the mites live in the dog's hair follicles and sebaceous glands in larger-than-normal numbers. This type of mange is commonly passed from the dam to her puppies and usually shows up on the puppies' muzzles, though demodicosis is not transferable from one normal dog to another. Most dogs recover from this type of mange without any treatment, though topical therapies are commonly prescribed by the vet.

The *Cheyletiellosis* mite is the hook-mouthed culprit associated with "walking dandruff," a condition that affects dogs as well as cats and rabbits. This mite lives on the surface of the animal's skin and is readily transferable through direct or indirect contact with an affected animal. The dandruff is present in the form of scaly skin, which may or may not be itchy. If not treated, this mange can affect a whole kennel of dogs and can be spread to humans as well.

The *Sarcoptes* mite causes intense itching on the dog in the form of a condition known as scabies or sarcoptic mange. The cycle of the *Sarcoptes* mite lasts about three weeks, and the mites live in the top layer of the dog's skin (epidermis), preferably in areas with little hair. Scabies is highly contagious and can be passed to humans. Sometimes an allergic reaction to the mite worsens the severe itching associated with sarcoptic mange.

Ear mites, *Otodectes cynotis,* lead to otodectic mange, which most commonly affects the outer ear canal of the dog, though other areas can be affected as well. Dogs with ear-mite infestation commonly scratch at their ears, causing further irritation, and shake their heads. Dark brown droppings in the outer ear confirm the diagnosis. Your vet can prescribe a treatment to flush out the ears and kill any eggs in the ears. A complete month of treatment is necessary to cure the mange.

Two other mites, less common in dogs, include *Dermanyssus gallinae* (the poultry or red mite) and *Eutrombicula alfreddugesi* (the North American mite associated with trombiculidiasis or chigger infestation). The poultry mite frequently lives on chickens, but can transfer to dogs who spend time near farm animals. Chigger

NOT A DROP TO DRINK
Never allow your dog to swim in polluted water or public areas where water quality can be suspect. Even perfectly clear water can harbor parasites, many of which can cause serious to fatal illnesses in canines. Areas inhabited by waterfowl and other wildlife are especially dangerous.

infestation affects dogs in the Central US who have exposure to woodlands. The types of mange caused by both of these mites are treatable by vets.

INTERNAL PARASITES
Most animals—fishes, birds and mammals, including dogs and humans—have worms and other parasites that live inside their bodies. According to Dr. Herbert R. Axelrod, the fish pathologist, there are two kinds of parasites: dumb and smart. The smart parasites live in peaceful cooperation with their hosts (symbiosis), while the dumb parasites kill their hosts. Most worm infections are relatively easy to control. If they are not controlled, they weaken the host dog to the point that other medical problems occur, but they do not kill the host as dumb parasites would.

A brown dog tick, *Rhipicephalus sanguineus*, is an uncommon but annoying tick found on dogs.
PHOTO BY CAROLINA BIOLOGICAL SUPPLY/PHOTOTAKE.

DO NOT MIX
Never mix parasite-control products without first consulting your vet. Some products can become toxic when combined with others and can cause fatal consequences.

The roundworm *Rhabditis* can infect both dogs and humans.

The roundworm, *Ascaris lumbricoides.*

ROUNDWORMS

Average-size dogs can pass 1,360,000 roundworm eggs every day. For example, if there were only 1 million dogs in the world, the world would be saturated with thousands of tons of dog feces. These feces would contain around 15,000,000,000 roundworm eggs.

Up to 31% of home yards and children's sand boxes in the US contain roundworm eggs.

Flushing dog's feces down the toilet is not a safe practice because the usual sewage treatments do not destroy roundworm eggs.

Infected puppies start shedding roundworm eggs at three weeks of age. They can be infected by their mother's milk.

ROUNDWORMS

The roundworms that infect dogs are known scientifically as *Toxocara canis*. They live in the dog's intestines and shed eggs continually. It has been estimated that a dog produces about 6 or more ounces of feces every day. Each ounce of feces averages hundreds of thousands of roundworm eggs. There are no known areas in which dogs roam that do not contain roundworm eggs. The greatest danger of roundworms is that they infect people, too! It is wise to have your dog tested regularly for roundworms.

In young puppies, roundworms cause bloated bellies, diarrhea, coughing and vomiting, and are transmitted from the dam (through blood or milk). Affected puppies will not appear as animated as normal puppies. The worms appear spaghetti-like, measuring as long as 6 inches. Adult dogs can acquire roundworms through coprophagia (eating contaminated feces) or by killing rodents that carry roundworms.

Roundworm infection can kill puppies and cause severe problems in adults, as the hatched larvae travel to the lungs and trachea through the bloodstream. Cleanliness is the best preventative for roundworms. Always pick up after your dog and dispose of feces in appropriate receptacles.

PHOTO BY DWIGHT R. KUHN.

HOOKWORMS

In the United States, dog owners have to be concerned about four different species of hookworm, the most common and most serious of which is *Ancylostoma caninum,* which prefers warm climates. The others are *Ancylostoma braziliense, Ancylostoma tubaeforme* and *Uncinaria stenocephala,* the latter of which is a concern to dogs living in the Northern US and Canada, as this species prefers cold climates. Hookworms are dangerous to humans as well as to dogs and cats, and can be the cause of severe anemia due to iron deficiency. The worm uses its teeth to attach itself to the dog's intestines and changes the site of its attachment about six times per day. Each time the worm repositions itself, the dog loses

blood and can become anemic. *Ancylostoma caninum* is the most likely of the four species to cause anemia in the dog.

Symptoms of hookworm infection include dark stools, weight loss, general weakness, pale coloration and anemia, as well as possible skin problems. Fortunately, hookworms are easily purged from the affected dog with a number of medications that have proven effective. Discuss these with your vet. Most heartworm preventatives include a hookworm insecticide as well.

Owners also must be aware that hookworms can infect humans, who can acquire the larvae through exposure to contaminated feces. Since the worms cannot complete their life cycle on a human, the worms simply infest the skin and cause irritation. This condition is known as cutaneous larva migrans syndrome. As a preventative, use disposable gloves or a "poop-scoop" to pick up your dog's droppings and prevent your dog (or neighborhood cats) from defecating in children's play areas.

The hookworm *Ancylostoma caninum.*

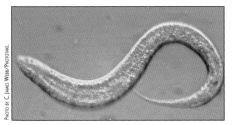

PHOTO BY C. JAMES WEBB/PHOTOTAKE.

The infective stage of the hookworm larva.

TAPEWORMS

Humans, rats, squirrels, foxes, coyotes, wolves and domestic dogs are all susceptible to tapeworm infection. Except in humans, tapeworms are usually not a fatal infection. Infected individuals can harbor 1,000 parasitic worms.

Tapeworms, like some other types of worm, are hermaphroditic, meaning male and female in the same worm.

If dogs eat infected rats or mice, or anything else infected with tapeworm, they get the tapeworm disease. One month after attaching to a dog's intestine, the worm starts shedding eggs. These eggs are infective immediately. Infective eggs can live for a few months without a host animal.

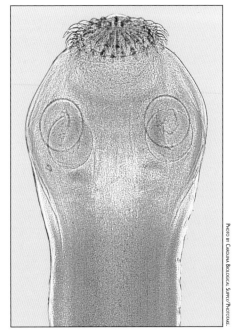

The head and rostellum (the round prominence on the scolex) of a tapeworm, which infects dogs and humans.

PHOTO BY CAROLINA BIOLOGICAL SUPPLY/PHOTOTAKE

TAPEWORMS

There are many species of tapeworm, all of which are carried by fleas! The most common tapeworm affecting dogs is known as *Dipylidium caninum*. The dog eats the flea and starts the tapeworm cycle. Humans can also be infected with tapeworms—so don't eat fleas! Fleas are so small that your dog could pass them onto your hands, your plate or your food and thus make it possible for you to ingest a flea that is carrying tapeworm eggs.

While tapeworm infection is not life-threatening in dogs (smart parasite!), it can be the cause of a very serious liver disease for humans. About 50% of the humans infected with *Echinococcus multilocularis*, a type of tapeworm that causes alveolar hydatid, perish.

WHIPWORMS

In North America, whipworms are counted among the most common parasitic worms in dogs. The whipworm's scientific name is *Trichuris vulpis*. These worms attach themselves in the lower parts of the intestine, where they feed. Affected dogs may only experience upset tummies, colic and diarrhea. These worms, however, can live for months or years in the dog, beginning their larval stage in the small intestine, spending their adult stage in the large intestine and finally passing infective eggs through the dog's feces. The only way to detect whipworms is through a fecal examination, though this is not always foolproof. Treatment for whipworms is tricky, due to the worms' unusual life-cycle pattern, and very often dogs are reinfected due to exposure to infective eggs on the ground. The whipworm eggs can survive in the environment for as long as five years, thus cleaning up droppings in your own backyard as well as in public places is absolutely essential for sanitation purposes and the health of your dog and others.

THREADWORMS

Though less common than round-worms, hookworms and those previously mentioned, thread-worms concern dog owners in the Southwestern US and Gulf Coast area where the climate is hot and humid. Living in the small intestine of the dog, this worm measures a mere 2 millimeters and is round in shape. Like that of the whipworm, the threadworm's life cycle is very complex and the eggs and larvae are passed through the feces. A deadly disease in humans, *Strongyloides* readily infects people, and the handling of feces is the most common means of transmission. Threadworms are most often seen in young puppies; bloody diarrhea and pneumonia are symptoms. Sick puppies must be isolated and treated immediately; vets recommend a follow-up treatment one month later.

HEARTWORM PREVENTATIVES

There are many heartworm preventatives on the market, many of which are sold at your veterinarian's office. These products can be given daily or monthly, depending on the manufacturer's instructions. All of these preventatives contain chemical insecticides directed at killing heartworms, which leads to some controversy among dog owners. In effect, heartworm preventatives are necessary evils, though you should determine how necessary based on your pet's lifestyle. There is no doubt that heartworm is a dreadful disease that threatens the life of dogs. However, the likelihood of your dog's being bitten by an infected mosquito is slim in most places, and a mosquito-repellent (or an herbal remedy such as Wormwood or Black Walnut) is much safer for your dog and will not compromise his immune system (the way heartworm preventatives will). Should you decide to use the traditional preventative "medications," you can consider giving the pill every other or third month. Since the toxins in the pill will kill the heartworms at all stages of development, the pill would be effective in killing larvae, nymphs or adults and it takes four months for the larvae to reach the adult stage. Thus, there is no rationale to poisoning the dog's system on a monthly basis. Lastly, do not give the pill during the winter months since there are no mosquitoes around to pass on their infection, unless you live in a tropical environment.

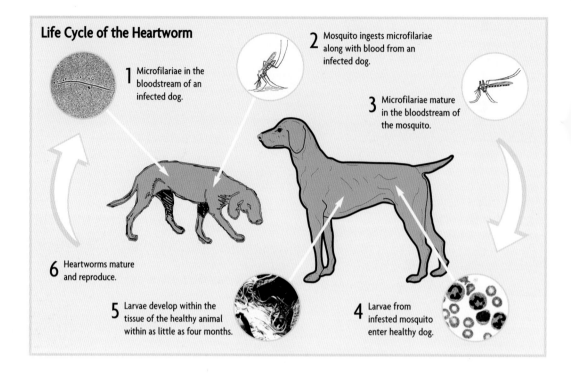

Life Cycle of the Heartworm

1 Microfilariae in the bloodstream of an infected dog.

2 Mosquito ingests microfilariae along with blood from an infected dog.

3 Microfilariae mature in the bloodstream of the mosquito.

6 Heartworms mature and reproduce.

5 Larvae develop within the tissue of the healthy animal within as little as four months.

4 Larvae from infested mosquito enter healthy dog.

HEARTWORMS

Heartworms are thin, extended worms up to 12 inches long, which live in a dog's heart and the major blood vessels surrounding it. Dogs may have up to 200 worms. Symptoms may be loss of energy, loss of appetite, coughing, the development of a pot belly and anemia.

Heartworms are transmitted by mosquitoes. The mosquito drinks the blood of an infected dog and takes in larvae with the blood. The larvae, called microfilariae, develop within the body of the mosquito and are passed on to the next dog bitten after the larvae mature. It takes two to three weeks for the larvae to develop to the infective stage within the body of the mosquito. Dogs are usually treated at about six weeks of age and maintained on a prophylactic dose given monthly.

Blood testing for heartworms is not necessarily indicative of how seriously your dog is infected. Although this is a dangerous disease, it is not easy for a dog to be infected. Discuss the various preventatives with your vet, as there are many different types now available. Together you can decide on a safe course of prevention for your dog.

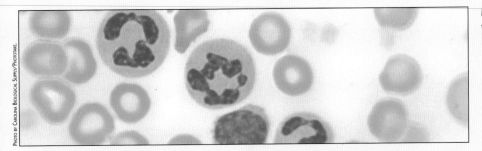

PHOTO BY CAROLINA BIOLOGICAL SUPPLY/PHOTOTAKE.

Magnified heart-worm larvae, *Dirofilaria immitis.*

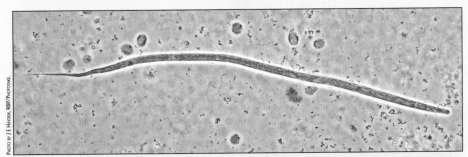

PHOTO BY J E HAYDEN, RBP/PHOTOTAKE.

Heartworm, *Dirofilaria immitis.*

PHOTO BY JAMES E. HAYDEN, RBP/PHOTOTAKE.

The heart of a dog infected with canine heartworm, *Dirofilaria immitis.*

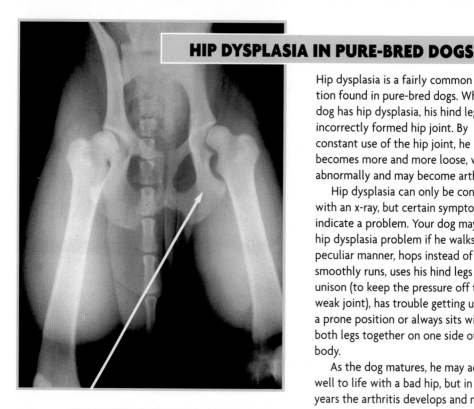

HIP DYSPLASIA IN PURE-BRED DOGS

Hip dysplasia is a fairly common condition found in pure-bred dogs. When a dog has hip dysplasia, his hind leg has an incorrectly formed hip joint. By constant use of the hip joint, he becomes more and more loose, wears abnormally and may become arthritic.

Hip dysplasia can only be confirmed with an x-ray, but certain symptoms may indicate a problem. Your dog may have a hip dysplasia problem if he walks in a peculiar manner, hops instead of smoothly runs, uses his hind legs in unison (to keep the pressure off the weak joint), has trouble getting up from a prone position or always sits with both legs together on one side of his body.

As the dog matures, he may adapt well to life with a bad hip, but in a few years the arthritis develops and many dogs with hip dysplasia become crippled.

Hip dysplasia is considered an inherited disease and can usually be diagnosed when the dog is three to nine months old, though two years of age is the benchmark for a dog to be definitely cleared as dysplasia-free. Some experts claim that a special diet might help your puppy outgrow the bad hip, but the usual treatments are surgical. The removal of the pectineus muscle, the removal of the round part of the femur, reconstructing the pelvis and replacing the hip with an artificial one are all surgical interventions that are expensive, but they are usually very successful. Follow the advice of your veterinarian.

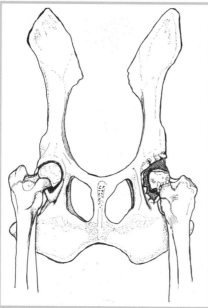

Hip dysplasia is a badly worn hip joint caused by improper fit of the bone into the socket. It is easily the most common hip problem in larger dogs, but dogs of any breed can be affected by hip dysplasia. The illustration shows a healthy hip joint on the left and an unhealthy hip joint on the right.

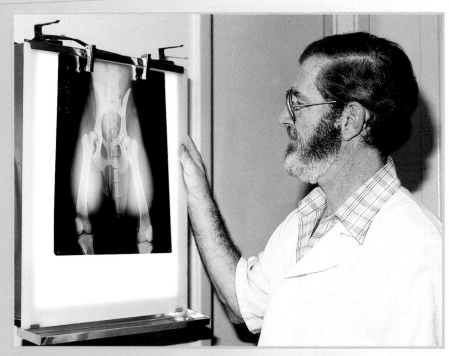

(Above) A veterinarian evaluating a dog's x-ray for hip dysplasia. Diagnosis can only be made using x-ray techniques, which are interpreted (read) by a suitably trained vet. (Below) The lateral (far left illustration) and flexed lateral (far right illustration) of a three-year-old dog's elbow manifesting elbow dysplasia with associated problems.

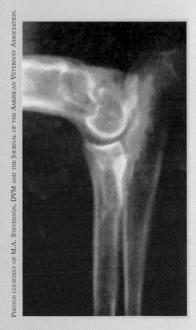

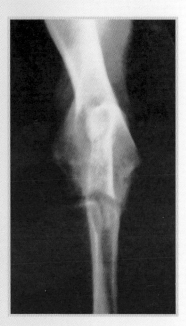

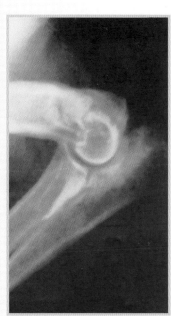

HOMEOPATHY:
an alternative
to conventional
medicine

"Less is Most"

Using this principle, the strength of a homeopathic remedy is measured by the number of serial dilutions that were undertaken to create it. The greater the number of serial dilutions, the greater the strength of the homeopathic remedy. The potency of a remedy that has been made by making a dilution of 1 part in 100 parts (or 1/100) is 1c or 1cH. If this remedy is subjected to a series of further dilutions, each one being 1/100, a more dilute and stronger remedy is produced. If the remedy is diluted in this way six times, it is called 6c or 6cH. A dilution of 6c is 1 part in 1,000,000,000,000. In general, higher potencies in more frequent doses are better for acute symptoms and lower potencies in more infrequent doses are more useful for chronic, long-standing problems.

CURING OUR DOGS NATURALLY

Holistic medicine means treating the whole animal as a unique, perfect living being. Generally, holistic treatments do not suppress the symptoms that the body naturally produces, as do most medications prescribed by conventional doctors and vets. Holistic methods seek to cure disease by regaining balance and harmony in the patient's environment. Some of these methods include use of nutritional therapy, herbs, flower essences, aromatherapy, acupuncture, massage, chiropractic and, of course, the most popular holistic approach, homeopathy.

Homeopathy is a theory or system of treating illness with small doses of substances which, if administered in larger quantities, would produce the symptoms that the patient already has. This approach is often described as "like cures like." Although modern veterinary medicine is geared toward the "quick fix," homeopathy relies on the belief that, given the time, the body is able to heal itself and return to its natural, healthy state.

Choosing a remedy to cure a problem in our dogs is the difficult part of homeopathy. Consult with your vet for a professional diagnosis of your dog's symptoms. Often

these symptoms require immediate conventional care. If your vet is willing and knowledgeable, you may attempt a homeopathic remedy. Be aware that cortisone prevents homeopathic remedies from working. There are hundreds of possibilities and combinations to cure many problems in dogs, from basic physical problems such as excessive shedding, fleas or other parasites, unattractive doggy odor, bad breath, upset tummy, obesity, dry, oily or dull coat, diarrhea, ear problems or eye discharge (including tears and dry or mucousy matter), to behavioral abnormalities such as fear of loud noises, habitual licking, poor appetite, excessive barking and various phobias. From alumina to zincum metallicum, the remedies span the planet and the imagination…from flowers and weeds to chemicals, insect droppings, diesel smoke and volcanic ash.

Using "Like to Treat Like"

Unlike conventional medicines that suppress symptoms, homeopathic remedies treat illnesses with small doses of substances that, if administered in larger quantities, would produce the symptoms that the patient already has. While the same homeopathic remedy can be used to treat different symptoms in different dogs, here are some interesting remedies and their uses.

Apis Mellifica
(made from honey bee venom) can be used for allergies or to reduce swelling that occurs in acutely infected kidneys.

Diesel Smoke
can be used to help control travel sickness.

Calcarea Fluorica
(made from calcium fluoride, which helps harden bone structure) can be useful in treating hard lumps in tissues.

Natrum Muriaticum
(made from common salt, sodium chloride) is useful in treating thin, thirsty dogs.

Nitricum Acidum
(made from nitric acid) is used for symptoms you would expect to see from contact with acids, such as lesions, especially where the skin joins the linings of body orifices or openings such as the lips and nostrils.

Symphytum
(made from the herb Knitbone, *Symphytum officianale*) is used to encourage bones to heal.

Urtica Urens
(made from the common stinging nettle) is used in treating painful, irritating rashes.

HOMEOPATHIC REMEDIES FOR YOUR DOG

Symptom/Ailment	Possible Remedy
ALLERGIES	Apis Mellifica 30c, Astacus Fluviatilis 6c, Pulsatilla 30c, Urtica Urens 6c
ALOPECIA	Alumina 30c, Lycopodium 30c, Sepia 30c, Thallium 6c
ANAL GLANDS (BLOCKED)	Hepar Sulphuris Calcareum 30c, Sanicula 6c, Silicea 6c
ARTHRITIS	Rhus Toxicodendron 6c, Bryonia Alba 6c
CATARACT	Calcarea Carbonica 6c, Conium Maculatum 6c, Phosphorus 30c, Silicea 30c
CONSTIPATION	Alumina 6c, Carbo Vegetabilis 30c, Graphites 6c, Nitricum Acidum 30c, Silicea 6c
COUGHING	Aconitum Napellus 6c, Belladonna 30c, Hyoscyamus Niger 30c, Phosphorus 30c
DIARRHEA	Arsenicum Album 30c, Aconitum Napellus 6c, Chamomilla 30c, Mercurius Corrosivus 30c
DRY EYE	Zincum Metallicum 30c
EAR PROBLEMS	Aconitum Napellus 30c, Belladonna 30c, Hepar Sulphuris 30c, Tellurium 30c, Psorinum 200c
EYE PROBLEMS	Borax 6c, Aconitum Napellus 30c, Graphites 6c, Staphysagria 6c, Thuja Occidentalis 30c
GLAUCOMA	Aconitum Napellus 30c, Apis Mellifica 6c, Phosphorus 30c
HEAT STROKE	Belladonna 30c, Gelsemium Sempervirens 30c, Sulphur 30c
HICCOUGHS	Cinchona Deficinalis 6c
HIP DYSPLASIA	Colocynthis 6c, Rhus Toxicodendron 6c, Bryonia Alba 6c
INCONTINENCE	Argentum Nitricum 6c, Causticum 30c, Conium Maculatum 30c, Pulsatilla 30c, Sepia 30c
INSECT BITES	Apis Mellifica 30c, Cantharis 30c, Hypericum Perforatum 6c, Urtica Urens 30c
ITCHING	Alumina 30c, Arsenicum Album 30c, Carbo Vegetabilis 30c, Hypericum Perforatum 6c, Mezerium 6c, Sulphur 30c
KENNEL COUGH	Drosera 6c, Ipecacuanha 30c
MASTITIS	Apis Mellifica 30c, Belladonna 30c, Urtica Urens 1m
MOTION SICKNESS	Cocculus 6c, Petroleum 6c
PATELLAR LUXATION	Gelsemium Sempervirens 6c, Rhus Toxicodendron 6c
PENIS PROBLEMS	Aconitum Napellus 30c, Hepar Sulphuris Calcareum 30c, Pulsatilla 30c, Thuja Occidentalis 6c
PUPPY TEETHING	Calcarea Carbonica 6c, Chamomilla 6c, Phytolacca 6c

CDS: COGNITIVE DYSFUNCTION SYNDROME
"Old-Dog Syndrome"

There are many ways for you to evaluate old-dog syndrome. Veterinarians have defined CDS (cognitive dysfunction syndrome) as the gradual deterioration of cognitive abilities. These are indicated by changes in the dog's behavior. When a dog changes his routine response, and maladies have been eliminated as the cause of these behavioral changes, then CDS is the usual diagnosis.

More than half the dogs over eight years old suffer from some form of CDS. The older the dog, the more chance it has of suffering from CDS. In humans, doctors often dismiss the CDS behavioral changes as part of "winding down."

There are four major signs of CDS: has frequent potty accidents inside the home, sleeping much more or much less than normal, acting confused and failure to respond to social stimuli.

SYMPTOMS OF CDS

FREQUENT POTTY ACCIDENTS
- *Urinates in the house.*
- *Defecates in the house.*
- *Doesn't signal that he wants to go out.*

SLEEP PATTERNS
- *Moves much more slowly.*
- *Sleeps more than normal during the day.*

CONFUSION
- *Goes outside and just stands there.*
- *Appears confused with a faraway look in his eyes.*
- *Hides more often.*
- *Doesn't recognize friends.*
- *Doesn't come when called.*
- *Sleeps less during the night.*
- *Walks around listlessly and without a destination.*

FAILING TO RESPOND TO SOCIAL STIMULI
- *Comes to people less frequently, whether called or not.*
- *Doesn't tolerate petting for more than a short time.*
- *Doesn't come to the door when you return home.*

Your Senior
BICHON FRISE

The term *old* is a qualitative term. For dogs, as well as their masters, old is relative. Certainly we can all distinguish between a puppy Bichon Frise and an adult Bichon Frise—there are the obvious physical traits, such as size, appearance and facial expressions, and personality traits. Puppies and young dogs like to play with children. Children's natural exuberance is a good match for the seemingly endless energy of young dogs. They like to run, jump, chase and retrieve. When dogs grow up and cease their interaction with children, they are often thought of as being too old to play with the kids.

On the other hand, if a Bichon Frise is only exposed to people with quieter life styles, his life will normally be less active and he will not seem to be getting old as his activity level slows down.

If people live to be 100 years old, dogs live to be 20 years old. While this is a good rule of thumb, it is very inaccurate. When trying to compare dog years to human years, you cannot make a generalization about all dogs. You can make the generalization that 15 years is a good lifespan for a Bichon Frise, which is quite good compared to, say, a Great Dane. Many large breeds typically live for fewer years than smaller ones. Dogs are generally considered mature within three years, but they can reproduce even earlier. So the first three years of a dog's life are like seven times that of comparable humans. That means a 3-year-old dog is like a 21-year-old human. As the curve of comparison shows, there is no hard and fast rule for comparing dog and human ages. The comparison is made even more difficult, for not all humans age at the same rate...and human females live longer than human males.

SENIOR SIGNS

An old dog starts to show one or more of the following symptoms:
- The hair on the face and paws starts to turn gray. The color breakdown usually starts around the eyes and mouth.
- Sleep patterns are deeper and longer, and the old dog is harder to awaken.
- Food intake diminishes.
- Responses to calls, whistles and other signals are ignored more and more.
- Eye contact does not evoke tail wagging (assuming it once did).

WHAT TO LOOK FOR IN SENIORS

Most veterinarians and behaviorists use the seven-year mark as the time to consider a dog a "senior." The term "senior" does not imply that the dog is geriatric and has begun to fail in mind and body. Aging is essentially a slowing process. Humans readily admit that they feel a difference in their activity level from age 20 to 30, and then from 30 to 40, etc. By treating the seven-year-old dog as a senior, owners are able to implement certain therapeutic and preventative medical strategies with the help of their veterinarians. A senior-care program should include at least two veterinary

visits per year, screening sessions to determine the dog's health status, as well as nutritional counseling. Vets determine the senior dog's health status through a blood smear for a complete blood count, serum chemistry profile with electrolytes, urinalysis, blood pressure check, electrocardiogram, ocular tonometry (pressure on the eyeball) and dental prophylaxis.

Such an extensive program for senior dogs is well advised before owners start to see the obvious physical signs of aging, such as slower and inhibited movement, graying, increased sleep/nap periods, and disinterest in play and other activity. This preventative program promises a longer, health-

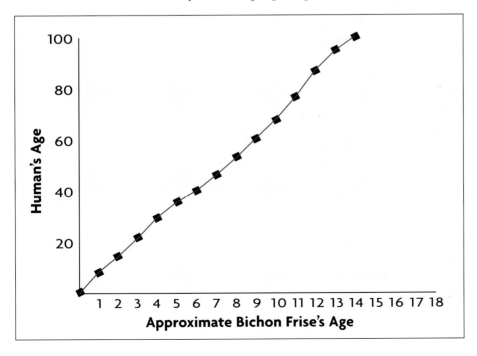

ier life for the aging dog. Among the physical problems common in aging dogs are the loss of sight and hearing, arthritis, kidney and liver failure, diabetes mellitus, heart disease and Cushing's disease (a hormonal disease).

In addition to the physical manifestations discussed, there are some behavioral changes and problems related to aging dogs. Dogs suffering from hearing or vision loss, dental discomfort or arthritis may become aggressive. Likewise the near-deaf and/or blind dog may

NOTICING THE SYMPTOMS

The symptoms listed below are symptoms that gradually appear and become more noticeable. They are not life-threatening; however, the symptoms below are to be taken very seriously and warrant a discussion with your veterinarian:

• Your dog cries and whimpers when he moves, and he stops running completely.

• Convulsions start or become more serious and frequent. The usual convulsion (spasm) is when the dog stiffens and starts to tremble, being unable or unwilling to move. The seizure usually lasts for 5 to 30 minutes.

• Your dog drinks more water and urinates more frequently. Wetting and bowel accidents take place indoors without warning.

• Vomiting becomes more and more frequent.

be startled more easily and react in an unexpectedly aggressive manner. Seniors suffering from senility can become more impatient and irritable. Housesoiling accidents are associated with loss of mobility, kidney problems, loss of sphincter control as well as plaque accumulation, physiological brain changes and reactions to medications. Older dogs, just like young puppies, suffer from separation anxiety, which may lead to excessive barking, whining, housesoiling and destructive behavior. Seniors may become fearful of everyday sounds, such as vacuum cleaners, heaters, thunder, and passing traffic. Some dogs have difficulty sleeping, due to discomfort, the need for frequent potty visits and the like. Owners should avoid spoiling the older dog with too many fatty treats. Obesity is a common problem in older dogs and subtracts years from their lives. Keep the senior dog as trim as possible since excessive weight puts additional stress on the body's vital organs. Some breeders recommend supplementing the diet with foods high in fiber and lower in calories. Adding fresh vegetables and marrow broth to the senior's diet makes a tasty, low-calorie, low-fat supplement. Vets also offer specialty diets for senior dogs that are worth exploring.

Your dog, as he nears his twilight years, needs his owner's patience and good care more than

WHEN YOUR DOG GETS OLD...
SIGNS THE OWNER CAN LOOK FOR

IF YOU NOTICE...	IT COULD INDICATE...
Discoloration of teeth and gums, foul breath, loss of appetite	Abcesses, gum disease, mouth lesions
Lumps, bumps, cysts, warts, fatty tumors	Cancers, benign or malignant
Cloudiness of eyes, apparent loss of sight	Cataracts, lenticular sclerosis, PRA, retinal dysplasia, blindness
Flaky coat, alopecia (hair loss)	Hormonal problems, hypothyroidism
Obesity, appetite loss, excessive weight gain	Various problems
Household accidents, increased urination	Diabetes, kidney or bladder disease
Increased thirst	Kidney disease, diabetes mellitus, bladder infection
Change in sleeping habits, coughing	Heart disease
Difficulty moving	Arthritis, degenerative joint disease, spondylosis (degenerative spine disease)

IF YOU NOTICE ANY OF THESE SIGNS, AN APPOINTMENT SHOULD BE MADE IMMEDIATELY WITH YOUR VETERINARIAN FOR A THOROUGH EVALUATION.

GETTING OLD
The bottom line is simply that your dog is getting old when you think he is getting old because he slows down in his level of general activity, including walking, running, eating, jumping and retrieving. On the other hand, the frequency of certain activities increases, such as more sleeping, more barking and more repetition of habits like going to the door without being called when you put your coat on to leave the house.

ever. Never punish an older dog for an accident or other abnormal behavior. For all the years of love, protection and companionship that your dog has provided, he deserves special attention and courtesies. The older dog may need to relieve himself at 3 a.m. because he can no longer hold it for eight hours. Older dogs may not be able to remain crated for more than two or three hours. It may be time to give up a sofa or chair to your old friend. Although he may not seem

as enthusiastic about your attention and petting, he does appreciate the considerations you offer as he gets older.

Your Bichon Frise does not understand why his world is slowing down. Owners must make the transition into the golden years as pleasant and rewarding as possible.

WHAT TO DO WHEN THE TIME COMES
You are never fully prepared to make a rational decision about putting your dog to sleep. It is very obvious that you love your Bichon Frise or you would not be reading this book. Putting a loved dog to sleep is extremely difficult. It is a decision that must be made with your veterinarian. You are usually forced to make the decision when one of the life-threatening symptoms listed above becomes serious enough for you to seek veterinary help.

If the prognosis of the malady indicates the end is near and your beloved pet will only suffer more and experience no enjoyment for the balance of his life, then euthanasia is the right choice.

WHAT IS EUTHANASIA?
Euthanasia derives from the Greek meaning *good death*. In other words, it means the planned, painless killing of a dog suffering from a painful, incurable condition, or who is so aged that he cannot

A resting place for your dog's ashes may be available locally. Contact you veterinarian or local dog club for information.

If you are interested in memorializing your dog, there are pet cemeteries that cater to pet lovers.

COPING WITH LOSS

When your dog dies, you may be as upset as when a human companion passes away. You are losing your protector, your baby, your confidante and your best friend. Many people experience not only grief but also feelings of guilt and doubt as to whether they did all that they could for their pet. Allow yourself to grieve and mourn, and seek help from friends and support groups. You may also wish to consult books and websites that deal with this topic.

walk, see, eat or control his excretory functions. Euthanasia is usually accomplished by injection with an overdose of an anesthesia or barbiturate. Aside from the prick of the needle, the experience is usually painless.

MAKING THE DECISION

The decision to euthanize your dog is never easy. The days during which the dog becomes ill and the end occurs can be unusually stressful for you. If this is your first experience with the death of a loved one, you may need the comfort dictated by your religious beliefs. If you are the head of the family and have children, you should have involved them in the decision of putting your Bichon Frise to sleep. Usually your dog can be maintained on drugs for a few days in order to give you ample time to make a decision. During this time, talking with members of your family or even people who have lived through this same experience can ease the burden.

THE FINAL RESTING PLACE

Dogs can have some of the same privileges as humans. They can occasionally be buried in their entirety in a pet cemetery which is generally expensive, or if they have died at home can be buried in your yard in a place suitably marked with some stone or newly planted tree or bush.
Alternatively they can be cremated and the ashes returned to you, or some people prefer to leave their dogs at the vet's to be disposed of.

All of these options should be discussed frankly and openly with your veterinarian. Do not be afraid to ask financial questions. Cremations can be individual, but a less expensive option is mass cremation, although of course the ashes can not then be returned. Vets can usually arrange cremation services on your behalf.

TALK IT OUT
The more openly your family discusses the whole stressful occurrence of the aging and eventual loss of a beloved pet, the easier it will be for you when the time comes.

GETTING ANOTHER DOG?

The grief of losing your beloved dog will be as lasting as the grief of losing a human friend or relative. In most cases, if your dog died of old age (if there is such a thing), he had slowed down considerably. Do you want a new Bichon puppy to replace it? Or are you better off in finding a more mature Bichon, say two to three years of age, which will usually be house-trained and will have an already developed personality. In this case, you can find out if you like each other after a few hours of being together.

The decision is, of course, your own. Do you want another Bichon Frise or perhaps a different breed so as to avoid comparison with your beloved friend? Most people usually buy the same breed because they know (and love) the characteristics of that breed. Then, too, they often know people who have the same breed and perhaps they are lucky enough that one of their friends expects a litter soon. What could be better?

Showing Your
BICHON FRISE

When you purchase your Bichon Frise, you will make it clear to the breeder whether you want one just as a lovable companion and pet, or if you hope to be buying a Bichon Frise with show prospects. No reputable breeder will sell you a young puppy and tell you that it is *definitely* of show quality, for so much can go wrong during the early months of a puppy's development. If you plan to show, what you will hopefully have acquired is a puppy with "show potential."

To the novice, exhibiting a Bichon Frise in the show ring may look easy, but it takes a lot of hard work and devotion to do top winning at a show such as the prestigious Westminster Kennel Club dog show, not to mention a little luck too!

The first concept that the canine novice learns when watching a dog show is that each dog first competes against members of his own breed. Once the judge has selected the best member of each breed (Best of Breed), provided that the show is judged on a Group system, that chosen dog will compete with other dogs in his group. Finally, the dogs chosen first in each group will compete for Best in Show.

The second concept that you must understand is that the dogs are not actually compared against one another. The judge compares each dog against his breed standard, the written description of the ideal specimen that is approved by the American Kennel Club (AKC). While some early breed standards were indeed based on specific dogs that were famous or popular, many dedicated enthusiasts say that a perfect specimen, as described in the standard, has never walked into a show ring, has never been bred and, to the woe of dog breeders around the globe, does not exist. Breeders attempt to get as close to this ideal as possible with every litter, but theoretically the "perfect" dog is so elusive that it is impossible.

Sometimes young people find great success and fun in handling their Bichons Frises on the show circuit. Dog showing and training is a very healthy outlet for juvenile exuberance.

Dog showing can be a very rewarding activity. Handlers and owners of top-quality dogs strive for the pride and prestige of winning in the show ring.

closest to you, contact the American Kennel Club, which furnishes the rules and regulations for all of these events plus general dog registration and other basic requirements of dog ownership.

The American Kennel Club offers three kinds of conformation shows. An all-breed show (for all AKC-recognized breeds), a specialty show (for one breed only, usually sponsored by the parent club) and a Group show (for all breeds in the Group).

For a dog to become an AKC champion of record, the dog must accumulate 15 points at the shows from at least three different judges, including two "majors." A "major" is defined as a three-, four- or five-point win, and the number of points per win is determined on the number of dogs entered in the show on the day. Depending on the breed, the number of points that are awarded varies. In a breed as popular as the Bichon Frise, more dogs are needed to rack up the points. At any dog show, only one dog and one bitch of each breed can win points.

Dog showing does not offer "co-ed" classes. Dogs and bitches never compete against each other in the classes. Non-champion dogs are called "class dogs" because they compete in one of five classes. Dogs are entered in a particular class depending on their age and previous show

(And if the "perfect" dog were born, breeders and judges would never agree that it was indeed "perfect.")

If you are interested in exploring the world of dog showing, your best bet is to join your local breed club or the national parent club, which is the Bichon Frise Club of America. These clubs often host both regional and national specialties, shows only for Bichons Frises, which can include conformation as well as obedience and agility trials. Even if you have no intention of competing with your Bichon Frise, a specialty is like a festival for lovers of the breed who congregate to share their favorite topic: Bichons Frises! Clubs also send out newsletters, and some organize training days and seminars in order that people may learn more about their chosen breed. To locate the breed club

MEET THE AKC

The American Kennel Club is the main governing body of the dog sport in the United States. Founded in 1884, the AKC consists of 500 or more independent dog clubs plus 4,500 affiliate clubs, all of which follow the AKC rules and regulations. Additionally, the AKC maintains a registry for pure-bred dogs in the US and works to preserve the integrity of the sport and its continuation in the country. Over 1,000,000 dogs are registered each year, representing about 150 recognized breeds. There are over 15,000 competitive events held annually for which over 2,000,000 dogs enter to participate. Dogs compete to earn over 40 different titles, from champion to Companion Dog to Master Agility Champion.

The judge at the show begins judging the Puppy Class, first dogs and then bitches, and proceeds through the classes. The judge places his winners first through fourth in each class. In the Winners Class, the first-place winners of each class compete with one another to determine Winners Dog and Winners Bitch. The judge also places a Reserve Winners Dog and Reserve Winners Bitch, which could be awarded the points in the case of a disqualification. The Winners Dog and Winners Bitch, the two that are awarded the points for the breed, then compete with any champions of record entered in

The winner and his trophies! Even the dog seems to be smiling about his successful day in the ring.

wins. To begin, there is the Puppy Class (for 6- to 9-month-olds and for 9- to 12-month-olds); this class is followed by the Novice Class (for dogs that have not won any first prizes except in the Puppy Class or three first prizes in the Novice Class and have not accumulated any points toward their champion title); the Bred-by-Exhibitor Class (for dogs handled by their breeders or handled by one of the breeder's immediate family); the American-bred Class (for dogs bred in the US!); and the Open Class (for any dog that is not a champion).

the show. The judge reviews the Winners Dog, Winners Bitch and all the other champions (often called "specials") to select his Best of Breed. The Best of Winners is selected between the Winners Dog and Winners Bitch. Were one of these two to be selected Best of Breed, it would automatically be named Best of Winners as well. Finally the judge selects his Best of Opposite Sex to the Best of Breed winner.

At a Group show or all-breed show, the Best of Breed winners from each breed then compete against one another for Group One through Group Four. The judge compares each Best of Breed to his breed standard, and the dog that most closely lives up to the ideal for his breed is selected as Group One. Finally, all seven group winners (from the Non-Sporting Group, Toy Group,

Behind the scenes at the Bichon benches during a large indoor show. There is a flurry of activity as the dogs are groomed to perfection before being presented in the ring.

Hound Group, etc.) compete for Best in Show.

To find out about dog shows in your area, you can subscribe to the American Kennel Club's monthly magazine, *The American Kennel Gazette* and the accompanying *Events Calendar*. You can also look in your local newspaper for advertisements for dog shows in your area or go on the Internet to the AKC's website, www.akc.org.

If your Bichon Frise is six months of age or older and registered with the AKC, you can enter him in a dog show where the breed is offered classes. Provided that your Bichon Frise does not have a disqualifying fault, he can compete. Only unaltered dogs can be entered in a dog show, so if you have spayed or neutered your Bichon Frise, your dog cannot compete in conformation shows. The reason for this is simple. Dog shows are the main forum to prove which representatives in a breed are worthy of being bred. Only dogs that have achieved championships—the AKC "seal of approval" for quality in pure-bred dogs—should be bred. Altered dogs, however, can participate in other AKC events such as obedience trials and the Canine Good Citizen program.

ENTERING A DOG SHOW
Before you actually step into the ring, you would be well advised

INFORMATION ON CLUBS
You can get information about dog shows from the national kennel clubs:

American Kennel Club
5580 Centerview Dr., Raleigh, NC 27606-3390
www.akc.org

United Kennel Club
100 E. Kilgore Road, Kalamazoo, MI 49002
www.ukcdogs.com

Canadian Kennel Club
89 Skyway Ave., Suite 100, Etobicoke, Ontario
M9W 6R4 Canada
www.ckc.ca

The Kennel Club
1-5 Clarges St., Piccadilly, London
W1Y 8AB, UK
www.the-kennel-club.org.uk

to sit back and observe the judge's ring procedure. If it is your first time in the ring, stand back and study how the exhibitor in front of you is performing. The judge asks each handler to "stack" the dog, hopefully showing the dog off to his best advantage. The judge will observe the dog from a distance and from different angles, and approach the dog to check his teeth, overall structure, alertness and muscle tone, as well as consider how well the dog "conforms" to the standard. Most importantly, the judge will have the exhibitor move the dog around the ring in some pattern that he should specify (always listen since some judges change their directions—and the judge is always right!). Finally, the judge will give the dog one last look before moving on to the next exhibitor.

If you are not in the top four in your class at your first show, do not be discouraged. Be patient and consistent, and you may eventually find yourself in a winning line-up. Remember that the winners were once in your shoes and have devoted many

Participating in dog shows can be a wonderful experience for dog and owner. If you have a good-quality Bichon Frise, do not be afraid to have it evaluated for showing.

hours and much money to earn the placement. If you find that your dog is losing every time and never getting a nod, it may be time to consider a different dog sport or to just enjoy your Bichon Frise as a pet. Parent clubs offer other events, such as agility, tracking, obedience, instinct tests and more, which may be of interest to the owner of a well-trained Bichon Frise.

OBEDIENCE TRIALS

Obedience trials in the US trace back to the early 1930s when organized obedience training was developed to demonstrate how well dog and owner could work together. The pioneer of obedience trials is Mrs. Helen Whitehouse Walker, a Standard Poodle fancier, who designed a series of exercises after the Associated Sheep, Police Army Dog Society of Great Britain. Since the days of Mrs. Walker, obedience trials have grown by leaps and bounds, and today there are over 2,000 trials held in the US every year, with more than 100,000 dogs competing. Any AKC-registered dog can enter an obedience trial, regardless of conformational disqualifications or neutering.

Obedience trials are divided into three levels of progressive difficulty. At the first level, the Novice, dogs compete for the title Companion Dog (CD); at the intermediate level, the Open, dogs

compete for the title Companion Dog Excellent (CDX); and at the advanced level, the Utility, dogs compete for the title Utility Dog (UD). Classes are sub-divided into "A" (for beginners) and "B" (for more experienced handlers). A perfect score at any level is 200, and a dog must score 170 or better to earn a "leg," of which three are needed to earn the title. To earn points, the dog must score more than 50% of the available points in each exercise; the possible points range from 20 to 40.

Each level consists of a different set of exercises. In the Novice level, the dog must heel on- and off-leash, come, long sit, long down and stand for examination. These skills are the basic ones required for a well-behaved "Companion Dog." The Open level requires that the dog perform the same exercises above but without a leash for extended lengths of time, as well as retrieve a dumbbell, broad jump and drop on recall. In the Utility level, dogs must perform ten difficult exercises, including scent discrimination, hand signals for basic commands, directed jump and directed retrieve.

Once a dog has earned the UD title, he can compete with other proven obedience dogs for the coveted title of Utility Dog Excellent (UDX), which requires that the dog win "legs" in ten shows.

Utility Dogs who earn "legs" in Open B and Utility B earn points toward their Obedience Trial Champion title. In 1977 the title Obedience Trial Champion (OTCh.) was established by the AKC. To become an OTCh., a dog needs to earn 100 points, which requires three first places in Open B and Utility under three different judges.

The Grand Prix of obedience trials, the AKC National Obedience Invitational gives qualifying Utility Dogs the chance to win the newest and highest title: National Obedience Champion (NOC). Only the top 25 ranked obedience dogs, plus any dog ranked in the top 3 in his breed, are allowed to compete.

AGILITY TRIALS

Having had its origins in the UK back in 1977, AKC agility had its official beginning in the US in August 1994, when the first licensed agility trials were held. The AKC allows all registered breeds (including Miscellaneous Class breeds) to participate, providing the dog is 12 months of age or older. Agility is designed so that the handler demonstrates how well the dog can work at his side. The handler directs his dog over an obstacle course that includes jumps as well as tires, the dog walk, weave poles, pipe tunnels, collapsed tunnels, etc. While working their way through

the course, the dog must keep one eye and ear on the handler and the rest of his body on the course. The handler gives verbal and hand signals to guide the dog through the course.

Agility is great fun for dog and owner with many rewards for everyone involved. Interested owners should join a training club that has obstacles and experienced agility handlers who can introduce you and your dog to the "ropes" (and tires, tunnels, etc.).

A wonderful combination of personality and beauty, the Bichon Frise is truly a "winner."

INDEX

My Bichon Frise

PUT YOUR PUPPY'S FIRST PICTURE HERE

Dog's Name _____

Date _____ Photographer _____